BURIAL SERVICES

Burial Services

Rite One and Rite Two

with The Holy Eucharist, Rite One and Rite Two
and Additional Material

compiled by

Joseph Buchanan Bernardin

Morehouse-Barlow Co., Inc.
Wilton, Connecticut
1980

Morehouse-Barlow Co., Inc.
78 Danbury Road
Wilton, Connecticut 06897

ISBN 0-8192-1267-9
Library of Congress Catalogue Card Number 79-87610

Printed in the United States of America

Acknowledgements

I wish to express my appreciation to the following for permission to use material copyrighted by them:

Scripture lessons used in the Rite II services. From *The New English Bible*. Copyright © The Delegates of the Oxford University Press and The Syndics of the Cambridge University Press 1961, 1970. Reprinted by permission.

"Burial of One Who Does Not Profess the Christian Faith." From *The Book of Occasional Services*. Copyright © The Church Pension Fund, New York, 1979. Reprinted by permission.

For all prayers marked [1] taken from *Prayers of the Spirit* by John Wallace Suter, published by Harper & Brothers, New York, 1943, and used by permission.

For all prayers marked [2] taken from *Joy in Believing*, selections from the words of Henry Sloane Coffin, edited by Walter Russell Bowie, © copyright 1956 Dorothy Prentice Coffin. Used by permission of Charles Scribner's Sons, New York.

Table of Contents

Preface

The 1979 Book of Common Prayer, in its section "The Burial of the Dead", contains much more material than that of 1928, part of which is to be found in previous editions of this present work. Nevertheless, there still remains a desire on the part of many clergymen to supplement the Prayer Book service to meet individual needs. Hence this completely revised edition, containing hopefully within one manageable book all the material needed for services at the time of death. In order not to make this book too large, the additional material, except for some modern services, is found only in traditional language.

The prayers, for the most part, are well known and familiar. I am under an immense debt to those who have given such helpful expression to their faith and hope in the presence of the death of those whom they love. In addition, I should like to express my gratitude to the many who, personally unknown to me, living or now dead, have composed prayers which have been used entire or altered in this compilation; and to the numerous friends who have given me prayers of their own or others' composition. As the original authors of many of the prayers are not known, at least to me, I crave their pardon if I have unwittingly used any material without proper permission.

J. B. BERNARDIN

Lent, A.D. *1980,*
Williamsburg, Virginia

Concerning the Service

The death of a member of the Church should be reported as soon as possible to, and arrangements for the funeral should be made in consultation with, the Minister of the Congregation.

Baptized Christians are properly buried from the church. The service should be held at a time when the congregation has opportunity to be present.

The coffin is to be closed before the service, and it remains closed thereafter. It is appropriate that it be covered with a pall or other suitable covering.

If necessary, or if desired, all or part of the service of Committal may be said in the church. If preferred, the Committal service may take place before the service in the church. It may also be used prior to cremation.

A priest normally presides at the service. It is appropriate that the bishop, when present, preside at the Eucharist and pronounce the Commendation.

It is desirable that the Lesson from the Old Testament, and the Epistle, be read by lay persons.

When the services of a priest cannot be obtained, a deacon or lay reader may preside at the service.

At the burial of a child, the passages from Lamentations, 1 John, and John 6, together with Psalm 23, are recommended.

It is customary that the celebrant meet the body and go before it into the church or towards the grave.

The anthems at the beginning of the service are sung or said as the body is borne into the church, or during the entrance of the ministers, or by the celebrant standing in the accustomed place.

The Burial of the Dead: Rite One

All stand while one or more of the following anthems are sung or said

I am the resurrection and the life, saith the Lord;
he that believeth in me, though he were dead, yet shall he live;
and whosoever liveth and believeth in me shall never die.

I know that my Redeemer liveth,
and that he shall stand at the latter day upon the earth;
and though this body be destroyed, yet shall I see God;
whom I shall see for myself and mine eyes shall behold,
and not as a stranger.

For none of us liveth to himself,
and no man dieth to himself.
For if we live, we live unto the Lord;
and if we die, we die unto the Lord.
Whether we live, therefore, or die, we are the Lord's.

Blessed are the dead who die in the Lord;
even so saith the Spirit, for they rest from their labors.

The Celebrant says one of the following Collects, first saying

The Lord be with you.
People   And with thy spirit.
Celebrant Let us pray.

At the Burial of an Adult

O God, whose mercies cannot be numbered: Accept our prayers on behalf of thy servant *N.*, and grant *him* an entrance into the land of light and joy, in the fellowship of thy saints; through Jesus Christ thy Son our Lord, who liveth and reigneth with thee and the Holy Spirit, one God, now and for ever. *Amen.*

At the Burial of a Child

O God, whose beloved Son did take little children into his arms and bless them: Give us grace, we beseech thee, to entrust this child *N.* to thy never-failing care and love, and bring us all to thy heavenly kingdom; through the same thy Son Jesus Christ our Lord, who liveth and reigneth with thee and the Holy Spirit, one God, now and for ever. *Amen.*

The people sit.

One or more of the following passages from Holy Scripture is read. If there is to be a Communion, a passage from the Gospel always concludes the Readings.

From the Old Testament

A Reading (Lesson) from _____.

A citation giving chapter and verse may be added.

Isaiah 25:6-9

In this mountain shall the LORD of hosts make unto all
people a feast of fat things, a feast of wines on the lees, of
fat things full of marrow, of wines on the lees well
refined. And he will destroy in this mountain the face of
the covering cast over all people, and the veil that is
spread over all nations. He will swallow up death in victory;
and the Lord GOD will wipe away tears from off all
faces; and the rebuke of his people shall be taken away from
off all the earth: for the LORD hath spoken it. And it
shall be said in that day, Lo, this is our God; we have
waited for him, and he will save us: this is the LORD: we
have waited for him, we will be glad and rejoice in his
salvation.

Isaiah 61:1-3

The Spirit of the Lord GOD is upon me; because the LORD
hath anointed me to preach good tidings unto the meek;
he hath sent me to bind up the brokenhearted,
to proclaim liberty to the captives, and the opening of the
prison to them that are bound; to proclaim the acceptable
year of the LORD, and the day of vengeance of our
God; to comfort all that mourn; to appoint unto them that
mourn in Zion, to give unto them beauty for ashes, the
oil of joy for mourning, the garment of praise for the
spirit of heaviness; that they might be called trees of
righteousness, the planting of the LORD, that he might be
glorified.

Lamentations 3:22-26, 31-33

It is of the LORD'S mercies that we are not consumed, because his compassions fail not. They are new every morning: great is thy faithfulness. The LORD is my portion, saith my soul; therefore will I hope in him. The LORD is good unto them that wait for him, to the soul that seeketh him. It is good that a man should both hope and quietly wait for the salvation of the LORD. For the Lord will not cast off for ever: but though he cause grief, yet will he have compassion according to the multitude of his mercies. For he doth not afflict willingly nor grieve the children of men.

Wisdom 3:1-5, 9

The souls of the righteous are in the hand of God, and there shall no torment touch them. In the sight of the unwise they seemed to die: and their departure is taken for misery, and their going from us to be utter destruction: but they are in peace. For though they be punished in the sight of men, yet is their hope full of immortality. And having been a little chastised, they shall be greatly rewarded: for God proved them, and found them worthy for himself. They that put their trust in him shall understand the truth: and such as be faithful in love shall abide with him: for grace and mercy is to his saints, and he hath care for his elect.

Job 19:21-27a

Have pity upon me, have pity upon me, O ye my friends;
for the hand of God hath touched me. Why do ye persecute
me as God, and are not satisfied with my flesh? Oh
that my words were now written! oh that they were printed
in a book! That they were graven with an iron pen and
lead in the rock for ever! For I know that my redeemer
liveth, and that he shall stand at the latter day upon
the earth: and though after my skin worms destroy this
body, yet in my flesh shall I see God: whom I shall
see for myself, and mine eyes shall behold, and not another.

After each Reading, the Reader may say

> The Word of the Lord.
People Thanks be to God.

or the Reader may say Here endeth the Reading.

*After the Old Testament Lesson, a suitable canticle or one of the
following Psalms may be sung or said*

Psalm 42 *Quemadmodum*

Like as the hart desireth the water-brooks, *
    so longeth my soul after thee, O God.

My soul is athirst for God, yea, even for the living God; *
    when shall I come to appear before the presence of God?

My tears have been my meat day and night, *
    while they daily say unto me, Where is now thy God?

Now when I think thereupon, I pour out my heart by myself; *
    for I went with the multitude, and brought them forth into
        the house of God;

In the voice of praise and thanksgiving, *
    among such as keep holy-day.

Why art thou so full of heaviness, O my soul? *
    and why art thou so disquieted within me?

O put thy trust in God; *
    for I will yet thank him, which is the help of my
                                countenance, and my God.

Psalm 46   *Deus noster refugium*

God is our hope and strength, *
    a very present help in trouble.

Therefore will we not fear, though the earth be moved, *
    and though the hills be carried into the midst of the sea;

Though the waters thereof rage and swell, *
    and though the mountains shake at the tempest of the same.

There is a river, the streams whereof make glad the city of God, *
    the holy place of the tabernacle of the Most Highest.

God is in the midst of her,
therefore shall she not be removed; *
    God shall help her, and that right early.

Be still then, and know that I am God; *
    I will be exalted among the nations,
    and I will be exalted in the earth.

The LORD of hosts is with us; *
    the God of Jacob is our refuge.

Psalm 90 *Domine, refugium*

Lord, thou hast been our refuge, *
 from one generation to another.

Before the mountains were brought forth,
or ever the earth and the world were made, *
 thou art God from everlasting, and world without end.

Thou turnest man to destruction; *
 again thou sayest, Come again, ye children of men.

For a thousand years in thy sight are but as yesterday
 when it is past, *
 and as a watch in the night.

As soon as thou scatterest them they are even as a sleep, *
 and fade away suddenly like the grass.

In the morning it is green, and groweth up; *
 but in the evening it is cut down, dried up, and withered.

For we consume away in thy displeasure, *
 and are afraid at thy wrathful indignation.

Thou hast set our misdeeds before thee, *
 and our secret sins in the light of thy countenance.

For when thou art angry all our days are gone; *
 we bring our years to an end, as it were a tale that is told.

The days of our age are threescore years and ten;
and though men be so strong that they come to fourscore years, *
 yet is their strength then but labor and sorrow,
 so soon passeth it away, and we are gone.

So teach us to number our days, *
 that we may apply our hearts unto wisdom.

p473

Psalm 121 *Levavi oculos*

I will lift up mine eyes unto the hills; *
   from whence cometh my help?

My help cometh even from the LORD, *
   who hath made heaven and earth.

He will not suffer thy foot to be moved, *
   and he that keepeth thee will not sleep.

Behold, he that keepeth Israel *
   shall neither slumber nor sleep.

The LORD himself is thy keeper; *
   the LORD is thy defense upon thy right hand;

So that the sun shall not burn thee by day, *
   neither the moon by night.

The LORD shall preserve thee from all evil; *
   yea, it is even he that shall keep thy soul.

The LORD shall preserve thy going out, and thy coming in, *
   from this time forth for evermore.

Psalm 130 *De profundis*

Out of the deep have I called unto thee, O LORD; *
   Lord, hear my voice.

O let thine ears consider well *
   the voice of my complaint.

If thou, LORD, wilt be extreme to mark what is done amiss, *
   O Lord, who may abide it?

For there is mercy with thee, *
   therefore shalt thou be feared.

I look for the LORD; my soul doth wait for him; *
    in his word is my trust.

My soul fleeth unto the Lord before the morning watch; *
    I say, before the morning watch.

O Israel, trust in the LORD,
for with the LORD there is mercy, *
    and with him is plenteous redemption.

And he shall redeem Israel *
    from all his sins.

Psalm 139 *Domine, probasti*

O LORD, thou hast searched me out, and known me. *
    Thou knowest my down-sitting and mine up-rising;
    thou understandest my thoughts long before.

Thou art about my path, and about my bed, *
    and art acquainted with all my ways.

For lo, there is not a word in my tongue, *
    but thou, O LORD, knowest it altogether.

Thou hast beset me behind and before, *
    and laid thine hand upon me.

Such knowledge is too wonderful and excellent for me; *
    I cannot attain unto it.

Whither shall I go then from thy Spirit? *
    or whither shall I go then from thy presence?

If I climb up into heaven, thou art there; *
    if I go down to hell, thou art there also.

If I take the wings of the morning, *
    and remain in the uttermost parts of the sea;

Even there also shall thy hand lead me, *
and thy right hand shall hold me.

If I say, Peradventure the darkness shall cover me, *
then shall my night be turned to day.

Yea, the darkness is no darkness with thee,
but the night is as clear as day; *
the darkness and light to thee are both alike.

From the New Testament

Romans 8:14-19, 34-35, 37-39

As many as are led by the Spirit of God, they are the
sons of God. For ye have not received the spirit of bondage
again to fear; but ye have received the Spirit of adoption,
whereby we cry, Abba, Father. The Spirit himself beareth
witness with our spirit, that we are the children of God;
and if children, then heirs; heirs of God, and joint-heirs
with Christ; if so be that we suffer with him, that we may
be also glorified together. For I reckon that the sufferings
of this present time are not worthy to be compared with
the glory which shall be revealed in us. For the earnest
expectation of the creature waiteth for the manifestation of
the sons of God. Who is he that condemneth? It is Christ
that died, yea rather, that is risen again, who is even
at the right hand of God, who also maketh intercession for
us. Who shall separate us from the love of Christ? shall
tribulation, or distress, or persecution, or famine, or
nakedness, or peril, or sword? Nay, in all these things we
are more than conquerors through him that loved us.
For I am persuaded, that neither death, nor life, nor angels,
nor principalities, nor powers, nor things present, nor
things to come, nor height, nor depth, nor any other
creature, shall be able to separate us from the love of God,
which is in Christ Jesus our Lord.

1 Corinthians 15:20-26, 35-38, 42-44, 53-58

But now is Christ risen from the dead, and become the
firstfruits of them that slept. For since by man came
death, by man came also the resurrection of the dead. For
as in Adam all die, even so in Christ shall all be made
alive. But every man in his own order: Christ the firstfruits;
afterward they that are Christ's at his coming. Then
cometh the end, when he shall have delivered up the
kingdom to God, even the Father; when he shall have put
down all rule and all authority and power. For he must
reign, till he hath put all enemies under his feet. The last
enemy that shall be destroyed is death. But some man will
say, How are the dead raised up? and with what body
do they come? Thou fool, that which thou sowest is not
quickened, except it die: and that which thou sowest, thou
sowest not that body that shall be, but bare grain, it
may chance of wheat, or of some other grain: but God
giveth it a body as it hath pleased him, and to every seed
his own body. So also is the resurrection of the dead.
It is sown in corruption; it is raised in incorruption: it is
sown in dishonor; it is raised in glory: it is sown in
weakness; it is raised in power: it is sown a natural body;
it is raised a spiritual body. There is a natural body,
and there is a spiritual body. For this corruptible must put
on incorruption, and this mortal must put on immortality.
So when this corruptible shall have put on incorruption,
and this mortal shall have put on immortality, then shall
be brought to pass the saying that is written, Death
is swallowed up in victory. O death, where is thy sting? O
grave, where is thy victory? The sting of death is sin;
and the strength of sin is the law. But thanks be to God,
which giveth us the victory through our Lord Jesus Christ.
Therefore, my beloved brethren, be ye steadfast, unmoveable,
always abounding in the work of the Lord, forasmuch
as ye know that your labor is not in vain in the Lord.

Burial of the Dead: Rite One   21

2 Corinthians 4:16—5:9

For which cause we faint not; but though our outward
man perish, yet the inward man is renewed day by day.
For our light affliction, which is but for a moment, worketh
for us a far more exceeding and eternal weight of glory;
while we look not at the things which are seen, but at
the things which are not seen: for the things which are seen
are temporal; but the things which are not seen are
eternal. For we know that if our earthly house of this
tabernacle were dissolved, we have a building of God, an
house not made with hands, eternal in the heavens. For
in this we groan, earnestly desiring to be clothed upon
with our house which is from heaven: if so be that being
clothed we shall not be found naked. For we that are
in this tabernacle do groan, being burdened: not for that
we would be unclothed, but clothed upon, that mortality
might be swallowed up of life. Now he that hath wrought
us for the selfsame thing is God, who also hath given
unto us the earnest of the Spirit. Therefore we are always
confident, knowing that, whilst we are at home in the
body, we are absent from the Lord: (for we walk by faith,
not by sight:) we are confident, I say, and willing rather
to be absent from the body, and to be present with the
Lord. Wherefore we labor, that, whether present or
absent, we may be accepted of him.

1 John 3:1-2

Behold, what manner of love the Father hath bestowed
upon us, that we should be called the sons of God:
therefore the world knoweth us not, because it knew him
not. Beloved, now are we the sons of God, and it doth not
yet appear what we shall be: but we know that, when
he shall appear, we shall be like him; for we shall see him
as he is.

Revelation 7:9-17

After this I beheld, and, lo, a great multitude, which no
man could number, of all nations, and kindreds, and
people, and tongues, stood before the throne, and before
the Lamb, clothed with white robes, and palms in their
hands; and cried with a loud voice, saying, Salvation
to our God which sitteth upon the throne, and unto the
Lamb. And all the angels stood round about the throne,
and about the elders and the four beasts, and fell before the
throne on their faces, and worshiped God, saying, Amen:
Blessing, and glory, and wisdom, and thanksgiving, and
honor, and power, and might, be unto our God for
ever and ever. Amen. And one of the elders answered,
saying unto me, What are these which are arrayed in
white robes? and whence came they? And I said unto him,
Sir, thou knowest. And he said to me, These are they
which came out of great tribulation, and have washed their
robes, and made them white in the blood of the Lamb.
Therefore are they before the throne of God, and serve
him day and night in his temple: and he that sitteth
on the throne shall dwell among them. They shall hunger
no more, neither thirst any more; neither shall the sun
light on them, nor any heat. For the Lamb which is in
the midst of the throne shall feed them, and shall lead them
unto living fountains of waters: and God shall wipe away
all tears from their eyes.

Revelation 21:2-7

And I John saw the holy city, new Jerusalem, coming down
from God out of heaven, prepared as a bride adorned
for her husband. And I heard a great voice out of heaven
saying, Behold, the tabernacle of God is with men, and he
will dwell with them, and they shall be his people, and
God himself shall be with them, and be their God. And God
shall wipe away all tears from their eyes; and there
shall be no more death, neither sorrow, nor crying, neither
shall there be any more pain: for the former things are
passed away. And he that sat upon the throne said, Behold,
I make all things new. And he said unto me, Write: for
these words are true and faithful. And he said unto me, It
is done. I am Alpha and Omega, the beginning and the
end. I will give unto him that is athirst of the fountain of
the water of life freely. He that overcometh shall inherit
all things; and I will be his God, and he shall be my son.

*After the New Testament Lesson, a suitable canticle or hymn, or one
of the following Psalms may be sung or said*

Psalm 23   *Dominus regit me*

The LORD is my shepherd; *
   therefore can I lack nothing.

He shall feed me in a green pasture, *
   and lead me forth beside the waters of comfort.

He shall convert my soul, *
   and bring me forth in the paths of righteousness for his
         Name's sake.

Yea, though I walk through the valley of the shadow of death
I will fear no evil; *
   for thou art with me;
   thy rod and thy staff comfort me.

Thou shalt prepare a table before me in the presence of them
        that trouble me; *
  thou hast anointed my head with oil,
  and my cup shall be full.

Surely thy loving-kindness and mercy shall follow me all the
        days of my life; *
  and I will dwell in the house of the LORD for ever.

Psalm 23   *King James Version*

p. 476

The LORD is my shepherd; *
  I shall not want.

He maketh me to lie down in green pastures; *
  he leadeth me beside the still waters.

He restoreth my soul; *
  he leadeth me in the paths of righteousness for his
        Name's sake.

Yea, though I walk through the valley of the shadow of death,
I will fear no evil; *
  for thou art with me;
  thy rod and thy staff, they comfort me.

Thou preparest a table before me in the presence of
        mine enemies; *
  thou anointest my head with oil;
  my cup runneth over.

Surely goodness and mercy shall follow me all the
        days of my life, *
  and I will dwell in the house of the LORD for ever.

Psalm 27 *Dominus illuminatio*

The LORD is my light and my salvation;
whom then shall I fear? *
    the LORD is the strength of my life;
    of whom then shall I be afraid?

One thing have I desired of the LORD, which I will require, *
    even that I may dwell in the house of the LORD all the
        days of my life,
    to behold the fair beauty of the LORD, and to visit his temple.

For in the time of trouble he shall hide me in his tabernacle;
    yea, in the secret place of his dwelling shall he hide me,
    and set me up upon a rock of stone.

And now shall he lift up mine head *
    above mine enemies round about me.

Therefore will I offer in his dwelling an oblation with
        great gladness: *
    I will sing and speak praises unto the LORD.

Hearken unto my voice, O LORD, when I cry unto thee; *
    have mercy upon me, and hear me.

My heart hath talked of thee, Seek ye my face. *
    Thy face, LORD, will I seek.

O hide not thou thy face from me, *
    nor cast thy servant away in displeasure.

I should utterly have fainted, *
    but that I believe verily to see the goodness of the LORD in
        the land of the living.

O tarry thou the LORD'S leisure; *
    be strong, and he shall comfort thine heart;
    and put thou thy trust in the LORD.

Psalm 106 *Confitemini Domino*

O give thanks unto the LORD, for he is gracious, *
and his mercy endureth for ever.

Who can express the noble acts of the LORD, *
or show forth all his praise?

Blessed are they that alway keep judgment, *
and do righteousness.

Remember me, O LORD, according to the favor that thou
bearest unto thy people; *
O visit me with thy salvation;

That I may see the felicity of thy chosen, *
and rejoice in the gladness of thy people,
and give thanks with thine inheritance.

Psalm 116 *Dilexi, quoniam*

My delight is in the LORD, *
because he hath heard the voice of my prayer;

Because he hath inclined his ear unto me, *
therefore will I call upon him as long as I live.

The snares of death compassed me round about, *
and the pains of hell gat hold upon me.

I found trouble and heaviness;
then called I upon the Name of the LORD; *
O LORD, I beseech thee, deliver my soul.

Gracious is the LORD, and righteous; *
yea, our God is merciful.

The LORD preserveth the simple; *
I was in misery, and he helped me.

Turn again then unto thy rest, O my soul, *
  for the LORD hath rewarded thee.

And why? thou hast delivered my soul from death, *
  mine eyes from tears, and my feet from falling.

I will walk before the LORD *
  in the land of the living.

I will pay my vows now in the presence of all his people; *
  right dear in the sight of the LORD is the death of his saints

The Gospel

*Then, all standing, the Deacon or Minister appointed reads the
Gospel, first saying*

> The Holy Gospel of our Lord Jesus Christ
> according to John.

People Glory be to thee, O Lord.

John 5:24-27

Verily, verily, I say unto you, He that heareth my word,
and believeth on him that sent me, hath everlasting life,
and shall not come into condemnation; but is passed
from death unto life. Verily, verily, I say unto you, The
hour is coming, and now is, when the dead shall hear
the voice of the Son of God: and they that hear shall live.
For as the Father hath life in himself; so hath he given
to the Son to have life in himself; and hath given him
authority to execute judgment also, because he is the Son
of man.

John 6:37-40

All that the Father giveth me shall come to me; and him
that cometh to me I will in no wise cast out. For I came
down from heaven, not to do mine own will, but the
will of him that sent me. And this is the Father's will which
hath sent me, that of all which he hath given me I should
lose nothing, but should raise it up again at the last
day. And this is the will of him that sent me, that every
one which seeth the Son, and believeth on him, may
have everlasting life: and I will raise him up at the last day.

John 10:11-16

I am the good shepherd: the good shepherd giveth his life
for the sheep. But he that is an hireling, and not the
shepherd, whose own the sheep are not, seeth the wolf
coming, and leaveth the sheep, and fleeth: and the wolf
catcheth them, and scattereth the sheep. The hireling
fleeth, because he is an hireling, and careth not for the
sheep. I am the good shepherd, and know my sheep, and
am known of mine. As the Father knoweth me, even
so know I the Father: and I lay down my life for the sheep.
And other sheep I have, which are not of this fold: them
also I must bring, and they shall hear my voice; and
there shall be one fold, and one shepherd.

John 11:21-27

Then said Martha unto Jesus, Lord, if thou hadst been
here, my brother had not died. But I know, that even now,
whatsoever thou wilt ask of God, God will give it thee.
Jesus saith unto her, Thy brother shall rise again. Martha
saith unto him, I know that he shall rise again in the
resurrection at the last day. Jesus said unto her, I am the
resurrection, and the life: he that believeth in me, though

he were dead, yet shall he live: and whosoever liveth and believeth in me shall never die. Believest thou this? She saith unto him, Yea, Lord: I believe that thou art the Christ, the Son of God, which should come into the world.

John 14:1-6

Let not your heart be troubled: ye believe in God, believe also in me. In my Father's house are many mansions: if it were not so, I would have told you. I go to prepare a place for you. And if I go and prepare a place for you, I will come again, and receive you unto myself; that where I am, there ye may be also. And whither I go ye know, and the way ye know. Thomas saith unto him, Lord, we know not whither thou goest; and how can we know the way? Jesus saith unto him, I am the way, the truth, and the life: no man cometh unto the Father, but by me.

At the end of the Gospel, the Reader says

> The Gospel of the Lord.
People Praise be to thee, O Christ.

A homily may be preached, the people being seated.

The Apostles' Creed may be said, all standing.

I believe in God, the Father almighty,
    maker of heaven and earth;
And in Jesus Christ his only Son our Lord;
    who was conceived by the Holy Ghost,
    born of the Virgin Mary,
    suffered under Pontius Pilate,
    was crucified, dead, and buried.
    He descended into hell.
    The third day he rose again from the dead.

He ascended into heaven,
and sitteth on the right hand of God the Father almighty.
From thence he shall come to judge the quick and the dead.
I believe in the Holy Ghost,
the holy catholic Church,
the communion of saints,
the forgiveness of sins,
the resurrection of the body,
and the life everlasting. Amen.

*If there is not to be a Communion, the Lord's Prayer is said here, and
the service continues with the following prayer of intercession, or
with one or more suitable prayers (see pages 40-42).*

Our Father, who art in heaven,
hallowed be thy Name,
thy kingdom come,
thy will be done,
on earth as it is in heaven.
Give us this day our daily bread.
And forgive us our trespasses,
as we forgive those who trespass against us.
And lead us not into temptation,
but deliver us from evil.
For thine is the kingdom, and the power, and the glory,
for ever and ever. Amen.

*When there is a Communion, the following serves for the Prayers of
the People.*

The People respond to every petition with Amen.

The Deacon or other leader says

In peace, let us pray to the Lord.

Almighty God, who hast knit together thine elect in one communion and fellowship, in the mystical body of thy Son Christ our Lord: Grant, we beseech thee, to thy whole Church in paradise and on earth, thy light and thy peace. *Amen.*

Grant that all who have been baptized into Christ's death and resurrection may die to sin and rise to newness of life, and that through the grave and gate of death we may pass with him to our joyful resurrection. *Amen.*

Grant to us who are still in our pilgrimage, and who walk as yet by faith, that thy Holy Spirit may lead us in holiness and righteousness all our days. *Amen.*

Grant to thy faithful people pardon and peace, that we may be cleansed from all our sins, and serve thee with a quiet mind. *Amen.*

Grant to all who mourn a sure confidence in thy fatherly care, that, casting all their grief on thee, they may know the consolation of thy love. *Amen.*

Give courage and faith to those who are bereaved, that they may have strength to meet the days ahead in the comfort of a reasonable and holy hope, in the joyful expectation of eternal life with those they love. *Amen.*

Help us, we pray, in the midst of things we cannot understand, to believe and trust in the communion of saints, the forgiveness of sins, and the resurrection to life everlasting. *Amen.*

Grant us grace to entrust *N.* to thy never-failing love; receive *him* into the arms of thy mercy, and remember *him* according to the favor which thou bearest unto thy people. *Amen.*

Grant that, increasing in knowledge and love of thee, *he* may go from strength to strength in the life of perfect service in thy heavenly kingdom. *Amen.*

Grant us, with all who have died in the hope of the resurrection, to have our consummation and bliss in thy eternal and everlasting glory, and, with [blessed *N.* and] all thy saints, to receive the crown of life which thou dost promise to all who share in the victory of thy Son Jesus Christ; who liveth and reigneth with thee and the Holy Spirit, one God, for ever and ever. *Amen.*

When there is no Communion, the service continues with the Commendation, or with the Committal.

At the Eucharist

The service continues with the Peace and the Offertory on page 43.

If the body is not present, the service continues with the [blessing and] dismissal.

The Commendation

Unless the Committal follows immediately in the church, the following Commendation is used.

Give rest, O Christ, to thy servant(s) with thy saints, where sorrow and pain are no more, neither sighing, but life everlasting.

Thou only art immortal, the creator and maker of mankind; and we are mortal, formed of the earth, and unto earth shall we return. For so thou didst ordain when thou createdst me, saying, "Dust thou art, and unto dust shalt thou return." All we go down to the dust; yet even at the grave we make our song: Alleluia, alleluia, alleluia.

Give rest, O Christ, to thy servant(s) with thy saints,
where sorrow and pain are no more,
neither sighing, but life everlasting.

The Celebrant, facing the body, says

Into thy hands, O merciful Savior, we commend thy servant
N. Acknowledge, we humbly beseech thee, a sheep of
thine own fold, a lamb of thine own flock, a sinner of
thine own redeeming. Receive *him* into the arms of thy
mercy, into the blessed rest of everlasting peace, and into
the glorious company of the saints in light. *Amen.*

The Celebrant, or the Bishop if present, may then bless the people,
and a Deacon or other Minister may dismiss them, saying

Let us go forth in the name of Christ.
Thanks be to God.

As the body is borne from the church, a hymn, or one or more of these
anthems may be sung or said

Christ is risen from the dead, trampling down death by
death, and giving life to those in the tomb.

The Sun of Righteousness is gloriously risen, giving light
to those who sat in darkness and in the shadow of death.

The Lord will guide our feet into the way of peace, having
taken away the sin of the world.

Christ will open the kingdom of heaven to all who believe
in his Name, saying, Come, O blessed of my Father; inherit
the kingdom prepared for you.

Into paradise may the angels lead thee; and at thy coming
may the martyrs receive thee, and bring thee into the holy
city Jerusalem.

or one of these Canticles

The Song of Zechariah *Benedictus*

Blessed be the Lord God of Israel, *
  for he hath visited and redeemed his people;

And hath raised up a mighty salvation for us *
  in the house of his servant David,

As he spake by the mouth of his holy prophets, *
  which have been since the world began:

That we should be saved from our enemies, *
  and from the hand of all that hate us;

To perform the mercy promised to our forefathers, *
  and to remember his holy covenant;

To perform the oath which he sware to our forefather Abraham, *
  that he would give us,

That we being delivered out of the hand of our enemies *
  might serve him without fear,

In holiness and righteousness before him, *
  all the days of our life.

And thou, child, shalt be called the prophet of the Highest, *
  for thou shalt go before the face of the Lord
      to prepare his ways;

To give knowledge of salvation unto his people *
  for the remission of their sins,

Through the tender mercy of our God, *
  whereby the dayspring from on high hath visited us;

To give light to them that sit in darkness
and in the shadow of death, *
  and to guide our feet into the way of peace.

The Song of Simeon   *Nunc dimittis*

Lord, now lettest thou thy servant depart in peace, *
   according to thy word;

For mine eyes have seen thy salvation, *
   which thou hast prepared before the face of all people,

To be a light to lighten the Gentiles, *
   and to be the glory of thy people Israel.

Christ our Passover   *Pascha nostrum*

Alleluia.
Christ our Passover is sacrificed for us, *
   therefore let us keep the feast,

Not with old leaven,
neither with the leaven of malice and wickedness, *
   but with the unleavened bread of sincerity and truth. Allelui

Christ being raised from the dead dieth no more; *
   death hath no more dominion over him.

For in that he died, he died unto sin once; *
   but in that he liveth, he liveth unto God.

Likewise reckon ye also yourselves to be dead indeed unto sin,
   but alive unto God through Jesus Christ our Lord. Alleluia

Christ is risen from the dead, *
   and become the first fruits of them that slept.

For since by man came death, *
   by man came also the resurrection of the dead.

For as in Adam all die, *
   even so in Christ shall all be made alive. Alleluia.

The Committal

The following anthem is sung or said

In the midst of life we are in death;
of whom may we seek for succor,
but of thee, O Lord,
who for our sins art justly displeased?

Yet, O Lord God most holy, O Lord most mighty,
O holy and most merciful Savior,
deliver us not into the bitter pains of eternal death.

Thou knowest, Lord, the secrets of our hearts;
shut not thy merciful ears to our prayer;
but spare us, Lord most holy, O God most mighty,
O holy and merciful Savior,
thou most worthy Judge eternal.
Suffer us not, at our last hour,
through any pains of death, to fall from thee.

or this

All that the Father giveth me shall come to me;
and him that cometh to me I will in no wise cast out.

He that raised up Jesus from the dead
will also give life to our mortal bodies,
by his Spirit that dwelleth in us.

Wherefore my heart is glad, and my spirit rejoiceth;
my flesh also shall rest in hope.

Thou shalt show me the path of life;
in thy presence is the fullness of joy,
and at thy right hand there is pleasure for evermore.

Then, while earth is cast upon the coffin, the Celebrant says these words

In sure and certain hope of the resurrection to eternal life through our Lord Jesus Christ, we commend to Almighty God our *brother N.*; and we commit *his* body to the ground;* earth to earth, ashes to ashes, dust to dust. The Lord bless *him* and keep *him*, the Lord make his face to shine upon *him* and be gracious unto *him*, the Lord lift up his countenance upon *him* and give *him* peace. *Amen.*

*Or the deep, *or* the elements, *or* its resting place.

The Celebrant says

> The Lord be with you.
>
> *People* And with thy spirit.
>
> *Celebrant* Let us pray.

Celebrant and People

Our Father, who art in heaven,
  hallowed be thy Name,
  thy kingdom come,
  thy will be done,
    on earth as it is in heaven.
Give us this day our daily bread.
And forgive us our trespasses,
  as we forgive those who trespass against us.
And lead us not into temptation,
  but deliver us from evil.
For thine is the kingdom, and the power, and the glory,
  for ever and ever. Amen.

Then the Celebrant may say

O Almighty God, the God of the spirits of all flesh, who
by a voice from heaven didst proclaim, Blessed are the
dead who die in the Lord: Multiply, we beseech thee, to
those who rest in Jesus the manifold blessings of thy love,
that the good work which thou didst begin in them may
be made perfect unto the day of Jesus Christ. And of thy
mercy, O heavenly Father, grant that we, who now serve
thee on earth, may at last, together with them, be partakers
of the inheritance of the saints in light; for the sake of
thy Son Jesus Christ our Lord. *Amen.*

*In place of this prayer, or in addition to it, the Celebrant may use
any of the Additional Prayers.*

Then may be said

Rest eternal grant to *him,* O Lord:
And let light perpetual shine upon him.

May *his* soul, and the souls of all the departed,
through the mercy of God, rest in peace. *Amen.*

The Celebrant dismisses the people with these words

The God of peace, who brought again from the dead our
Lord Jesus Christ, the great Shepherd of the sheep, through
the blood of the everlasting covenant: Make you perfect
in every good work to do his will, working in you that
which is well pleasing in his sight; through Jesus Christ, to
whom be glory for ever and ever. *Amen.*

The Consecration of a Grave

*If the grave is in a place that has not previously been set apart for
Christian burial, the Priest may use the following prayer, either
before the service of Committal or at some other convenient time*

O God, whose blessed Son was laid in a sepulcher in the garden: Bless, we pray, this grave, and grant that *he* whose body is (is to be) buried here may dwell with Christ in paradise, and may come to thy heavenly kingdom; through thy Son Jesus Christ our Lord. *Amen.*

Additional Prayers

Almighty and everlasting God, we yield unto thee most high praise and hearty thanks for the wonderful grace and virtue declared in all thy saints, who have been the choice vessels of thy grace, and the lights of the world in their several generations; most humbly beseeching thee to give us grace so to follow the example of their steadfastness in thy faith, and obedience to thy holy commandments, that at the day of the general resurrection, we, with all those who are of the mystical body of thy Son, may be set on his right hand, and hear that his most joyful voice: "Come, ye blessed of my Father, inherit the kingdom prepared for you from the foundation of the world." Grant this, O Father, for the sake of the same thy Son Jesus Christ, our only Mediator and Advocate. *Amen.*

Almighty God, with whom do live the spirits of those who depart hence in the Lord, and with whom the souls of the faithful, after they are delivered from the burden of the flesh, are in joy and felicity: We give thee hearty thanks for the good examples of all those thy servants, who, having finished their course in faith, do now rest from their labors. And we beseech thee that we, with all those who are departed in the true faith of thy holy Name, may have our perfect consummation and bliss, both in body and soul, in thy eternal and everlasting glory; through Jesus Christ our Lord. *Amen.*

Into thy hands, O Lord, we commend thy servant *N.*, our dear *brother*, as into the hands of a faithful Creator and most merciful Savior, beseeching thee that *he* may be precious in thy sight. Wash *him*, we pray thee, in the blood of that immaculate Lamb that was slain to take away the sins of the world; that, whatsoever defilements *he* may have contracted in the midst of this earthly life being purged and done away, *he* may be presented pure and without spot before thee; through the merits of Jesus Christ thine only Son our Lord. *Amen.*

Remember thy servant, O Lord, according to the favor which thou bearest unto thy people; and grant that, increasing in knowledge and love of thee, *he* may go from strength to strength in the life of perfect service in thy heavenly kingdom; through Jesus Christ our Lord. *Amen.*

Almighty God, our heavenly Father, in whose hands are the living and the dead: We give thee thanks for all thy servants who have laid down their lives in the service of our country. Grant to them thy mercy and the light of thy presence; and give us such a lively sense of thy righteous will, that the work which thou hast begun in them may be perfected; through Jesus Christ thy Son our Lord. *Amen.*

O God, whose days are without end, and whose mercies cannot be numbered: Make us, we beseech thee, deeply sensible of the shortness and uncertainty of life; and let thy Holy Spirit lead us in holiness and righteousness all our days; that, when we shall have served thee in our generation, we may be gathered unto our fathers, having the testimony of a good conscience; in the communion of the Catholic Church; in the confidence of a certain faith; in the comfort of a reasonable, religious, and holy hope; in favor with thee our God; and in perfect charity with the world. All which we ask through Jesus Christ our Lord. *Amen.*

O God, the King of saints, we praise and magnify thy holy Name for all thy servants who have finished their course in thy faith and fear; for the blessed Virgin Mary; for the holy patriarchs, prophets, apostles, and martyrs; and for all other thy righteous servants, known to us and unknown; and we beseech thee that, encouraged by their examples, aided by their prayers, and strengthened by their fellowship, we also may be partakers of the inheritance of the saints in light; through the merits of thy Son Jesus Christ our Lord. *Amen.*

O Lord Jesus Christ, Son of the living God, we pray thee to set thy passion, cross, and death, between thy judgment and our souls, now and in the hour of our death. Give mercy and grace to the living, pardon and rest to the dead, to thy holy Church peace and concord, and to us sinners everlasting life and glory; who with the Father and the Holy Spirit livest and reignest, one God, now and for ever. *Amen.*

Almighty God, Father of mercies and giver of all comfort: Deal graciously, we pray thee, with all those who mourn, that casting every care on thee, they may know the consolation of thy love; through Jesus Christ our Lord. *Amen.*

The Holy Eucharist: Rite One

The Peace

All stand. The Celebrant says to the people

The peace of the Lord be always with you.
People And with thy spirit.

Then the Ministers and People may greet one another in the name of the Lord.

The Holy Communion

The Celebrant may begin the Offertory with some appropriate sentence of Scripture.

Ascribe to the Lord the honor due his Name; bring offerings and come into his courts. *Psalm 96:8*

During the Offertory, a hymn, psalm, or anthem may be sung.

Representatives of the congregation bring the people's offerings of bread and wine to the deacon or celebrant. The people stand while the offerings are presented and placed on the Altar.

The Great Thanksgiving

Eucharistic Prayer I

The people remain standing. The Celebrant, whether bishop or priest, faces them and sings or says

The Lord be with you.
People And with thy spirit.
Celebrant Lift up your hearts.
People We lift them up unto the Lord.
Celebrant Let us give thanks unto our Lord God.
People It is meet and right so to do.

Then, facing the Holy Table, the Celebrant proceeds

It is very meet, right, and our bounden duty, that we should at all times, and in all places, give thanks unto thee, O Lord, holy Father, almighty, everlasting God, through Jesus Christ our Lord; who rose victorious from the dead, and doth comfort us with the blessed hope of everlasting life; for to thy faithful people, O Lord, life is changed, not ended; and when our mortal body doth lie in death, there is prepared for us a dwelling place eternal in the heavens. Therefore with Angels and Archangels, and with all the company of heaven, we laud and magnify thy glorious Name; evermore praising thee, and saying,

Celebrant and People

Holy, holy, holy, Lord God of Hosts:
Heaven and earth are full of thy glory.
Glory be to thee, O Lord Most High.

Here may be added

Blessed is he that cometh in the name of the Lord.
Hosanna in the highest.

The people kneel or stand.

Then the Celebrant continues

All glory be to thee, Almighty God, our heavenly Father,
for that thou, of thy tender mercy, didst give thine only
Son Jesus Christ to suffer death upon the cross for our
redemption; who made there, by his one oblation of
himself once offered, a full, perfect, and sufficient sacrifice,
oblation, and satisfaction, for the sins of the whole world;
and did institute, and in his holy Gospel command us
to continue, a perpetual memory of that his precious death
and sacrifice, until his coming again.

*At the following words concerning the bread, the Celebrant is to
hold it, or lay a hand upon it; and at the words concerning the cup,
to hold or place a hand upon the cup and any other vessel containing
wine to be consecrated.*

For in the night in which he was betrayed, he took bread;
and when he had given thanks, he brake it, and gave it
to his disciples, saying, "Take, eat, this is my Body, which
is given for you. Do this in remembrance of me."

Likewise, after supper, he took the cup; and when he had
given thanks, he gave it to them, saying, "Drink ye all
of this; for this is my Blood of the New Testament, which
is shed for you, and for many, for the remission of sins.
Do this, as oft as ye shall drink it, in remembrance of me."

Wherefore, O Lord and heavenly Father, according to the
institution of thy dearly beloved Son our Savior Jesus
Christ, we, thy humble servants, do celebrate and make
here before thy divine Majesty, with these thy holy gifts,
which we now offer unto thee, the memorial thy Son
hath commanded us to make; having in remembrance his
blessed passion and precious death, his mighty resurrection

and glorious ascension; rendering unto thee most hearty thanks for the innumerable benefits procured unto us by the same.

And we most humbly beseech thee, O merciful Father, to hear us; and, of thy almighty goodness, vouchsafe to bless and sanctify, with thy Word and Holy Spirit, these thy gifts and creatures of bread and wine; that we, receiving them according to thy Son our Savior Jesus Christ's holy institution, in remembrance of his death and passion, may be partakers of his most blessed Body and Blood.

And we earnestly desire thy fatherly goodness mercifully to accept this our sacrifice of praise and thanksgiving; most humbly beseeching thee to grant that, by the merits and death of thy Son Jesus Christ, and through faith in his blood, we, and all thy whole Church, may obtain remission of our sins, and all other benefits of his passion.

And here we offer and present unto thee, O Lord, our selves, our souls and bodies, to be a reasonable, holy, and living sacrifice unto thee; humbly beseeching thee that we, and all others who shall be partakers of this Holy Communion, may worthily receive the most precious Body and Blood of thy Son Jesus Christ, be filled with thy grace and heavenly benediction, and made one body with him, that he may dwell in us, and we in him.

And although we are unworthy, through our manifold sins, to offer unto thee any sacrifice, yet we beseech thee to accept this our bounden duty and service, not weighing our merits, but pardoning our offenses, through Jesus Christ our Lord;

By whom, and with whom, in the unity of the Holy Ghost, all honor and glory be unto thee, O Father Almighty, world without end. *AMEN.*

And now, as our Savior Christ hath taught us, we are
bold to say,

People and Celebrant

Our Father, who art in heaven,
    hallowed be thy Name,
    thy kingdom come,
    thy will be done,
        on earth as it is in heaven.
Give us this day our daily bread.
And forgive us our trespasses,
    as we forgive those who trespass against us.
And lead us not into temptation,
    but deliver us from evil.
For thine is the kingdom, and the power, and the glory,
    for ever and ever. Amen.

The Breaking of the Bread

The Celebrant breaks the consecrated Bread.

A period of silence is kept.

Then may be sung or said

[Alleluia.] Christ our Passover is sacrificed for us;
Therefore let us keep the feast. [Alleluia.]

*In Lent, Alleluia is omitted, and may be omitted at other times except
during Easter Season.*

The following or some other suitable anthem may be sung or said here

O Lamb of God, that takest away the sins of the world,
have mercy upon us.
O Lamb of God, that takest away the sins of the world,
have mercy upon us.

O Lamb of God, that takest away the sins of the world, grant us thy peace.

The following prayer may be said. The People may join in saying this prayer

We do not presume to come to this thy Table, O merciful Lord, trusting in our own righteousness, but in thy manifold and great mercies. We are not worthy so much as to gather up the crumbs under thy Table. But thou art the same Lord whose property is always to have mercy. Grant us therefore, gracious Lord, so to eat the flesh of thy dear Son Jesus Christ, and to drink his blood, that we may evermore dwell in him, and he in us. *Amen.*

Facing the people, the Celebrant may say the following Invitation

The Gifts of God for the People of God.
and may add Take them in remembrance that Christ died for you, and feed on him in your hearts by faith, with thanksgiving.

The ministers receive the Sacrament in both kinds, and then immediately deliver it to the people.

The Bread and the Cup are given to the communicants with these words

The Body of our Lord Jesus Christ, which was given for thee, preserve thy body and soul unto everlasting life. Take and eat this in remembrance that Christ died for thee, and feed on him in thy heart by faith, with thanksgiving.

The Blood of our Lord Jesus Christ, which was shed for thee, preserve thy body and soul unto everlasting life. Drink this in remembrance that Christ's Blood was shed for thee, and be thankful.

or with these words

The Body (Blood) of our Lord Jesus Christ keep you in everlasting life. [*Amen.*]

or with these words

The Body of Christ, the bread of heaven. [*Amen.*]
The Blood of Christ, the cup of salvation. [*Amen.*]

During the ministration of Communion, hymns, psalms, or anthems may be sung.

When necessary, the Celebrant consecrates additional bread and wine.

After Communion, the Celebrant says

Let us pray.

The People may join in saying this prayer

Almighty God, we thank thee that in thy great love thou hast fed us with the spiritual food and drink of the Body and Blood of thy Son Jesus Christ, and hast given unto us a foretaste of thy heavenly banquet. Grant that this Sacrament may be unto us a comfort in affliction, and a pledge of our inheritance in that kingdom where there is no death, neither sorrow nor crying, but the fullness of joy with all thy saints; through Jesus Christ our Savior. *Amen.*

The service continues with the Commendation or Committal, page 33 or 37, if the body is not present, the service continues with the [blessing and] dismissal.

The Bishop when present, or the Priest, gives the blessing

The peace of God, which passeth all understanding, keep your hearts and minds in the knowledge and love of God,

and of his Son Jesus Christ our Lord; and the blessing
of God Almighty, the Father, the Son, and the Holy Ghost,
be amongst you, and remain with you always. *Amen.*

or this

The blessing of God Almighty, the Father, the Son, and
the Holy Spirit, be upon you and remain with you for
ever. *Amen.*

The Deacon, or the Celebrant, may dismiss the people with these words

Let us go forth in the name of Christ.
People Thanks be to God.

or the following

Deacon Go in peace to love and serve the Lord.
People Thanks be to God.

or this

Deacon Let us go forth into the world, rejoicing in the
power of the Spirit.
People Thanks be to God.

or this

Deacon Let us bless the Lord.
People Thanks be to God.

*From the Easter Vigil through the Day of Pentecost "Alleluia, alleluia"
may be added to any of the dismissals.*

The People respond Thanks be to God. Alleluia, alleluia.

The Burial of the Dead: Rite Two

p. 491

All stand while one or more of the following anthems are sung or said. A hymn, psalm, or some other suitable anthem may be sung instead.

I am Resurrection and I am Life, says the Lord.
Whoever has faith in me shall have life,
even though he die.
And everyone who has life,
and has committed himself to me in faith,
shall not die for ever.

As for me, I know that my Redeemer lives
and that at the last he will stand upon the earth.
After my awaking, he will raise me up;
and in my body I shall see God.
I myself shall see, and my eyes behold him
who is my friend and not a stranger.

For none of us has life in himself,
and none becomes his own master when he dies.
For if we have life, we are alive in the Lord,
and if we die, we die in the Lord.
So, then, whether we live or die,
we are the Lord's possession.

Happy from now on
are those who die in the Lord!
So it is, says the Spirit,
for they rest from their labors.

Or else this anthem

In the midst of life we are in death;
from whom can we seek help?
From you alone, O Lord,
who by our sins are justly angered.

Holy God, Holy and Mighty,
Holy and merciful Savior,
deliver us not into the bitterness of eternal death.

Lord, you know the secrets of our hearts;
shut not your ears to our prayers,
but spare us, O Lord.

Holy God, Holy and Mighty,
Holy and merciful Savior,
deliver us not into the bitterness of eternal death.

O worthy and eternal Judge,
do not let the pains of death
turn us away from you at our last hour.

Holy God, Holy and Mighty,
Holy and merciful Savior,
deliver us not into the bitterness of eternal death.

When all are in place, the Celebrant may address the congregation,
acknowledging briefly the purpose of their gathering, and bidding
their prayers for the deceased and the bereaved.

p. 493

The Celebrant then says

The Lord be with you.
People   And also with you.
Celebrant Let us pray.

Silence may be kept; after which the Celebrant says one of the following Collects

At the Burial of an Adult

O God, who by the glorious resurrection of your Son Jesus Christ destroyed death, and brought life and immortality to light: Grant that your servant N., being raised with him, may know the strength of his presence, and rejoice in his eternal glory; who with you and the Holy Spirit lives and reigns, one God, for ever and ever. *Amen.*

or this

O God, whose mercies cannot be numbered: Accept our prayers on behalf of your servant N., and grant *him* an entrance into the land of light and joy, in the fellowship of your saints; through Jesus Christ our Lord, who lives and reigns with you and the Holy Spirit, one God, now and for ever. *Amen.*

or this

O God of grace and glory, we remember before you this day our brother (sister) N. We thank you for giving *him* to us, *his* family and friends, to know and to love as a companion on our earthly pilgrimage. In your boundless compassion, console us who mourn. Give us faith to see in death the gate of eternal life, so that in quiet confidence we may continue our course on earth, until, by your call, we are reunited with those who have gone before; through Jesus Christ our Lord. *Amen.*

At the Burial of a Child

O God, whose beloved Son took children into his arms and blessed them: Give us grace to entrust *N.* to your never-failing care and love, and bring us all to your heavenly kingdom; through Jesus Christ our Lord, who lives and reigns with you and the Holy Spirit, one God, now and for ever. *Amen.*

The Celebrant may add the following prayer

Most merciful God, whose wisdom is beyond our understanding: Deal graciously with *NN.* in *their* grief. Surround *them* with your love, that *they* may not be overwhelmed by *their* loss, but have confidence in your goodness, and strength to meet the days to come; through Jesus Christ our Lord. *Amen.*

The people sit.

One or more of the following passages from Holy Scripture is read. If there is to be a Communion, a passage from the Gospel always concludes the Readings.

The Liturgy of the Word

From the Old Testament

Isaiah 25:6-9

On this mountain the LORD of Hosts will prepare a banquet of rich fare for all the peoples, a banquet of wines well matured and richest fare, well-matured wines strained clear. On this mountain the LORD will swallow up that veil that shrouds all the peoples, the pall thrown over all the

nations; he will swallow up death for ever. Then the Lord
GOD will wipe away the tears from every face and remove
the reproach of his people from the whole earth. The
LORD has spoken. On that day men will say, See, this is
our God for whom we have waited to deliver us; this
is the LORD for whom we have waited; let us rejoice and
exult in his deliverance.

Isaiah 61:1-3

The spirit of the Lord GOD is upon me because the LORD
has anointed me; he has sent me to bring good news to
the humble, to bind up the broken-hearted, to proclaim
liberty to captives and release to those in prison; to
proclaim a year of the LORD'S favour and a day of the
vengeance of our God; to comfort all who mourn, to
give them garlands instead of ashes, oil of gladness instead
of mourners' tears, a garment of splendour for the heavy
heart. They shall be called Trees of Righteousness, planted
by the LORD for his glory.

Lamentations 3:22-26, 31-33

The LORD'S true love is surely not spent, nor has his
compassion failed; they are new every morning, so great is
his constancy. The LORD, I say, is all that I have; therefore
I will wait for him patiently. The LORD is good to those
who look for him, to all who seek him; it is good to
wait in patience and sigh for deliverance by the LORD. For
the Lord will not cast off his servants for ever. He may
punish cruelly, yet he will have compassion in the fullness
of his love; he does not willingly afflict or punish any
mortal man.

Wisdom 3:1-5, 9

But the souls of the just are in God's hand, and torment
shall not touch them. In the eyes of foolish men they
seemed to be dead; their departure was reckoned as defeat,
and their going from us as disaster. But they are at peace,
for though in the sight of men they may be punished,
they have a sure hope of immortality; and after a little
chastisement they will receive great blessings, because God
has tested them and found them worthy to be his. Those
who have put their trust in him shall understand that
he is true, and the faithful shall attend upon him in love;
they are his chosen, and grace and mercy shall be theirs.

Job 19:21-27a

Pity me, pity me, you that are my friends; for the hand of
God has touched me. Why do you pursue me as God
pursues me? Have you not had your teeth in me long enough?
O that my words might be inscribed, O that they might
be engraved in an inscription, cut with an iron tool and
filled with lead to be a witness in hard rock! But in my
heart I know that my vindicator lives and that he will
rise last to speak in court; and I shall discern my witness
standing at my side and see my defending counsel, even
God himself, whom I shall see with my own eyes.

*A suitable psalm, hymn, or canticle may follow. The following Psalms
are appropriate:*

Psalm 42   *Quemadmodum*

As the deer longs for the water-brooks, *
   so longs my soul for you, O God.

My soul is athirst for God, athirst for the living God; *
   when shall I come to appear before the presence of God?

My tears have been my food day and night, *
    while all day long they say to me,
    "Where now is your God?"

I pour out my soul when I think on these things: *
    how I went with the multitude and led them into the
        house of God,

With the voice of praise and thanksgiving, *
    among those who keep holy-day.

Why are you so full of heaviness, O my soul? *
    and why are you so disquieted within me?

Put your trust in God; *
    for I will yet give thanks to him,
    who is the help of my countenance, and my God.

Psalm 46   *Deus noster refugium*

God is our refuge and strength, *
    a very present help in trouble.

Therefore we will not fear, though the earth be moved, *
    and though the mountains be toppled into the
        depths of the sea;

Though its waters rage and foam, *
    and though the mountains tremble at its tumult.

The LORD of hosts is with us; *
    the God of Jacob is our stronghold.

There is a river whose streams make glad the city of **God**, *
    the holy habitation of the Most High.

God is in the midst of her;
she shall not be overthrown; *
    God shall help her at the break of day.

"Be still, then, and know that I am God; *
   I will be exalted among the nations;
   I will be exalted in the earth."

The LORD of hosts is with us; *
   the God of Jacob is our stronghold.

Psalm 90 *Domine, refugium*

Lord, you have been our refuge *
   from one generation to another.

Before the mountains were brought forth,
or the land and the earth were born, *
   from age to age you are God.

You turn us back to the dust and say, *
   "Go back, O child of earth."

For a thousand years in your sight are like yesterday
                  when it is past *
   and like a watch in the night.

You sweep us away like a dream; *
   we fade away suddenly like the grass.

In the morning it is green and flourishes; *
   in the evening it is dried up and withered.

For we consume away in your displeasure; *
   we are afraid because of your wrathful indignation.

Our iniquities you have set before you, *
   and our secret sins in the light of your countenance.

When you are angry, all our days are gone; *
   we bring our years to an end like a sigh.

The span of our life is seventy years,
perhaps in strength even eighty; *
    yet the sum of them is but labor and sorrow,
    for they pass away quickly and we are gone.

Who regards the power of your wrath? *
    who rightly fears your indignation?

So teach us to number our days *
    that we may apply our hearts to wisdom.

Psalm 121   *Levavi oculos*

I lift up my eyes to the hills; *
    from where is my help to come?

My help comes from the LORD, *
    the maker of heaven and earth.

He will not let your foot be moved *
    and he who watches over you will not fall asleep.

Behold, he who keeps watch over Israel *
    shall neither slumber nor sleep;

The LORD himself watches over you; *
    the LORD is your shade at your right hand,

So that the sun shall not strike you by day, *
    nor the moon by night.

The LORD shall preserve you from all evil; *
    it is he who shall keep you safe.

The LORD shall watch over your going out and
                  your coming in, *
    from this time forth for evermore.

Psalm 130 *De profundis*

Out of the depths have I called to you, O LORD;
Lord, hear my voice; *
　　let your ears consider well the voice of my supplication.

If you, LORD, were to note what is done amiss, *
　　O Lord, who could stand?

For there is forgiveness with you; *
　　therefore you shall be feared.

I wait for the LORD; my soul waits for him; *
　　in his word is my hope.

My soul waits for the Lord,
more than watchmen for the morning, *
　　more than watchmen for the morning.

O Israel, wait for the LORD, *
　　for with the LORD there is mercy;

With him there is plenteous redemption, *
　　and he shall redeem Israel from all their sins.

Psalm 139 *Domine, probasti*

LORD, you have searched me out and known me; *
　　you know my sitting down and my rising up;
　　you discern my thoughts from afar.

You trace my journeys and my resting-places *
　　and are acquainted with all my ways.

Indeed, there is not a word on my lips, *
　　but you, O LORD, know it altogether.

You press upon me behind and before *
　　and lay your hand upon me.

Such knowledge is too wonderful for me; *
   it is so high that I cannot attain to it.

Where can I go then from your Spirit? *
   where can I flee from your presence?

If I climb up to heaven, you are there; *
   if I make the grave my bed, you are there also.

If I take the wings of the morning *
   and dwell in the uttermost parts of the sea,

Even there your hand will lead me *
   and your right hand hold me fast.

If I say, "Surely the darkness will cover me, *
   and the light around me turn to night,"

Darkness is not dark to you;
the night is as bright as the day; *
   darkness and light to you are both alike.

From the New Testament

Romans 8:14-19, 34-35, 37-39

For all who are moved by the Spirit of God are sons of
God. The Spirit you have received is not a spirit of slavery
leading you back into a life of fear, but a Spirit that
makes us sons, enabling us to cry 'Abba! Father!' In that
cry the Spirit of God joins with our spirit in testifying
that we are God's children; and if children, then heirs. We
are God's heirs and Christ's fellow-heirs, if we share his
sufferings now in order to share his splendour hereafter.
For I reckon that the sufferings we now endure bear no
comparison with the splendour, as yet unrevealed, which

is in store for us. For the created universe waits with eager expectation for God's sons to be revealed. It is Christ —Christ who died, and, more than that, was raised from the dead—who is at God's right hand, and indeed pleads our cause. Then what can separate us from the love of Christ? Can affliction or hardship? Can persecution, hunger, nakedness, peril, or the sword? And yet, in spite of all, overwhelming victory is ours through him who loved us. For I am convinced that there is nothing in death or life, in the realm of spirits or superhuman powers, in the world as it is or the world as it shall be, in the forces of the universe, in heights or depths—nothing in all creation that can separate us from the love of God in Christ Jesus our Lord.

1 Corinthians 15:20-26, 35-38, 42-44, 53-58

But the truth is, Christ was raised to life—the firstfruits of the harvest of the dead. For since it was a man who brought death into the world, a man also brought resurrection of the dead. As in Adam all men die, so in Christ all will be brought to life; but each in his own proper place: Christ the firstfruits, and afterwards, at his coming, those who belong to Christ. Then comes the end, when he delivers up the kingdom to God the Father, after abolishing every kind of domination, authority, and power. For he is destined to reign until God has put all enemies under his feet; and the last enemy to be abolished is death. But, you may ask, how are the dead raised? In what kind of body? How foolish! The seed you sow does not come to life unless it has first died; and what you sow is not the body that shall be, but a naked grain, perhaps of wheat, or of some other kind; and God clothes it with the body of his choice, each seed with its own particular body. So it is with the resurrection of the dead. What is sown in the earth as a perishable thing is raised imperishable. Sown in humiliation, it is raised in glory; sown in weakness, it is raised in power; sown as an animal body, it is raised as a spiritual body. If there is such a thing as an animal body, there is also a spiritual body. This perishable being must be clothed with the imperishable, and what is mortal must be clothed with immortality. And when our mortality has been clothed with immortality, then the saying of Scripture will come true: 'Death is swallowed up; victory is won! O Death, where is your victory? O Death, where is your sting?' The sting of death is sin, and sin gains its power from the law; but, God be praised, he gives us the victory through our Lord Jesus Christ. Therefore,my beloved brothers, stand firm and immovable, and work for the Lord always, work without limit, since you know that in the Lord your labour cannot be lost.

2 Corinthians 4:16—5:9

No wonder we do not lose heart! Though our outward humanity is in decay, yet day by day we are inwardly renewed. Our troubles are slight and short-lived; and their outcome an eternal glory which outweighs them far. Meanwhile our eyes are fixed, not on the things that are seen, but on the things that are unseen: for what is seen passes away; what is unseen is eternal. For we know that if the earthly frame that houses us today should be demolished, we possess a building which God has provided —a house not made by human hands, eternal, and in heaven. In this present body we do indeed groan; we yearn to have our heavenly habitation put on over this one— in the hope that, being thus clothed, we shall not find ourselves naked. We groan indeed, we who are enclosed within this earthly frame; we are oppressed because we do not want to have the old body stripped off. Rather our desire is to have the new body put on over it, so that our mortal part may be absorbed into life immortal. God himself has shaped us for this very end; and as a pledge of it he has given us the Spirit. Therefore we never cease to be confident. We know that so long as we are at home in the body we are exiles from the Lord; faith is our guide, we do not see him. We are confident, I repeat, and would rather leave our home in the body and go to live with the Lord. We therefore make it our ambition, wherever we are, here or there, to be acceptable to him.

1 John 3:1-2

How great is the love that the Father has shown to us! We were called God's children, and such we are; and the reason why the godless world does not recognize us is that it has not known him. Here and now, dear friends, we are God's children; what we shall be has not yet been disclosed, but we know that when it is disclosed we shall be like him, because we shall see him as he is.

Revelation 7:9-17

After this I looked and saw a vast throng, which no one could count, from every nation, of all tribes, peoples, and languages, standing in front of the throne and before the Lamb. They were robed in white and had palms in their hands, and they shouted together: 'Victory to our God who sits on the throne, and to the Lamb!' And all the angels stood round the throne and the elders and the four living creatures, and they fell on their faces before the throne and worshiped God, crying: 'Amen! Praise and glory and wisdom, thanksgiving and honour, power and

might, be to our God for ever and ever! Amen.' Then
one of the elders turned to me and said, 'These men that
are robed in white—who are they and from where do
they come?' But I answered, 'My Lord, you know, not I.'
Then he said to me, 'These are the men who have passed
through the great ordeal; they have washed their robes and
made them white in the blood of the Lamb. That is why
they stand before the throne of God and minister to him
day and night in his temple; and he who sits on the throne
will dwell with them. They shall never again feel hunger
or thirst, the sun shall not beat on them nor any scorching
heat, because the Lamb who is at the heart of the throne
will be their shepherd and will guide them to the springs of
the water of life; and God will wipe all tears from their
eyes.'

Revelation 21:2-7

I saw the holy city, new Jerusalem, coming down out of
heaven from God, made ready like a bride adorned for her
husband. I heard a loud voice proclaiming from the
throne: 'Now at last God has his dwelling among men! He
will dwell among them and they shall be his people, and
God himself will be with them. He will wipe every tear
from their eyes; there shall be an end to death, and to
mourning and crying and pain; for the old order has
passed away!' Then he who sat on the throne said, 'Behold!
I am making all things new!' (And he said to me, 'Write
this down; for these words are trustworthy and true.
Indeed they are already fulfilled.') 'I am the Alpha and the
Omega, the beginning and the end. A draught from the
water-springs of life will be my free gift to the thirsty.
All this is the victor's heritage; and I will be his God and
he shall be my son.'

A suitable psalm, hymn, or canticle may follow. The following Psalms are appropriate:

Psalm 23 *Dominus regit me*

The LORD is my shepherd; *
  I shall not be in want.

He makes me lie down in green pastures *
  and leads me beside still waters.

He revives my soul *
  and guides me along right pathways for his Name's sake.

Though I walk through the valley of the shadow of death,
I shall fear no evil; *
    for you are with me;
    your rod and your staff, they comfort me.

You spread a table before me in the presence of those
                    who trouble me; *
    you have anointed my head with oil,
    and my cup is running over.

Surely your goodness and mercy shall follow me all the days
                    of my life, *
  and I will dwell in the house of the LORD for ever.

Psalm 27 *Dominus illuminatio*

The LORD is my light and my salvation;
whom then shall I fear? *
    the LORD is the strength of my life;
    of whom then shall I be afraid?

One thing have I asked of the LORD;
one thing I seek; *
    that I may dwell in the house of the LORD all the days
                    of my life;

To behold the fair beauty of the LORD *
and to seek him in his temple.

For in the day of trouble he shall keep me safe in his shelter; *
he shall hide me in the secrecy of his dwelling
and set me high upon a rock.

Even now he lifts up my head *
above my enemies round about me.

Therefore I will offer in his dwelling an oblation
with sounds of great gladness; *
I will sing and make music to the LORD.

Hearken to my voice, O LORD, when I call; *
have mercy on me and answer me.

You speak in my heart and say, "Seek my face." *
Your face, LORD, will I seek.

Hide not your face from me, *
nor turn away your servant in displeasure.

What if I had not believed
that I should see the goodness of the LORD *
in the land of the living!

O tarry and await the LORD'S pleasure;
be strong, and he shall comfort your heart; *
wait patiently for the LORD.

Psalm 106 *Confitemini Domino*

Hallelujah!
Give thanks to the LORD, for he is good, *
for his mercy endures for ever.

Who can declare the mighty acts of the LORD *
or show forth all his praise?

Happy are those who act with justice *
  and always do what is right!

Remember me, O LORD, with the favor you have
                  for your people, *
  and visit me with your saving help;

That I may see the prosperity of your elect
and be glad with the gladness of your people, *
  that I may glory with your inheritance.

Psalm 116   *Dilexi, quoniam*

I love the LORD, because he has heard the voice of my
                  supplication, *
  because he has inclined his ear to me whenever I
                  called upon him.

The cords of death entangled me;
the grip of the grave took hold of me; *
  I came to grief and sorrow.

Then I called upon the Name of the LORD: *
  "O LORD, I pray you, save my life."

Gracious is the LORD and righteous; *
  our God is full of compassion.

The LORD watches over the innocent; *
  I was brought very low, and he helped me.

Turn again to your rest, O my soul, *
  for the LORD has treated you well.

For you have rescued my life from death, *
  my eyes from tears, and my feet from stumbling.

I will walk in the presence of the LORD *
  in the land of the living.

I will fulfill my vows to the LORD *
  in the presence of all his people.

Precious in the sight of the LORD *
  is the death of his servants.

The Gospel

Then, all standing, the Deacon or Minister appointed reads the Gospel, first saying

> The Holy Gospel of our Lord Jesus Christ
> according to John.

People Glory to you, Lord Christ.

John 5:24-27

'In very truth, anyone who gives heed to what I say and puts his trust in him who sent me has hold of eternal life, and does not come up for judgment, but has already passed from death to life. In truth, in very truth I tell you, a time is coming, indeed it is already here, when the dead shall hear the voice of the Son of God, and all who hear shall come to life. For as the Father has life-giving power in himself, so has the Son, by the Father's gift. As Son of Man, he has also been given the right to pass judgment.'

√ John 6:37-40

'All that the Father gives me will come to me, and the man who comes to me I will never turn away. I have come down from heaven, not to do my own will, but the will of him who sent me. It is his will that I should not lose even one of all that he has given me, but raise them all up on the last day. For it is my Father's will that everyone who looks upon the Son and puts his faith in him shall possess eternal life; and I will raise him up on the last day.'

John 10:11-16

'I am the good shepherd; the good shepherd lays down his life for the sheep. The hireling, when he sees the wolf coming, abandons the sheep and runs away, because he is no shepherd and the sheep are not his. Then the wolf harries the flock and scatters the sheep. The man runs away because he is a hireling and cares nothing for the sheep. I am the good shepherd; I know my own sheep and my sheep know me—as the Father knows me and I know the Father—and I lay down my life for the sheep. But there are other sheep of mine, not belonging to this fold, whom I must bring in; and they too will listen to my voice. There will then be one flock, one shepherd.'

John 11:21-27

Martha said to Jesus, 'If you had been here, sir, my brother would not have died. Even now I know that whatever you ask of God, God will grant you.' Jesus said, 'Your brother will rise again.' 'I know that he will rise again,' said Martha, 'at the resurrection on the last day.' Jesus said, 'I am the resurrection and I am life. If a man has faith in me, even though he die, he shall come to life; and no one who is alive and has faith shall ever die. Do you believe this?' 'Lord, I do,' she answered; 'I now believe that you are the Messiah, the Son of God who was to come into the world.'

John 14:1-6

'Set your troubled hearts at rest. Trust in God always; trust also in me. There are many dwelling-places in my Father's house; if it were not so I should have told you; for I am going there on purpose to prepare a place for you. And if I go and prepare a place for you, I shall come again

and receive you to myself, so that where I am you may
be also; and my way there is known to you.' Thomas said,
'Lord, we do not know where you are going, so how can
we know the way?' Jesus replied, 'I am the way; I am the
truth and I am life; no one comes to the Father except
by me.'

At the end of the Gospel, the Reader says

    The Gospel of the Lord.
People Praise to you, Lord Christ.

*Here there may be a homily by the Celebrant, or a member of the
family, or a friend.*

*The Apostles' Creed may then be said, all standing. The Celebrant
may introduce the Creed with these or similar words*

In the assurance of eternal life given at Baptism, let us
proclaim our faith and say,

Celebrant and People   P. 496

I believe in God, the Father almighty,
   creator of heaven and earth.

I believe in Jesus Christ, his only Son, our Lord.
   He was conceived by the power of the Holy Spirit
      and born of the Virgin Mary.
   He suffered under Pontius Pilate,
      was crucified, died, and was buried.
   He descended to the dead.
   On the third day he rose again.
   He ascended into heaven,
      and is seated at the right hand of the Father.
   He will come again to judge the living and the dead.

I believe in the Holy Spirit,
   the holy catholic Church,
   the communion of saints,

the forgiveness of sins,
the resurrection of the body,
and the life everlasting. Amen.

*If there is not to be a Communion, the Lord's Prayer is said here, and
the service continues with the Prayers of the People, or with one or
more suitable prayers (see pages 78-80).*

*When there is a Communion, the following form of the Prayers of the
People is used, or else the form on page 198 or pages 31-33.*

For our brother (sister) N., let us pray to our Lord Jesus
Christ who said, "I am Resurrection and I am Life."

Lord, you consoled Martha and Mary in their distress;
draw near to us who mourn for N., and dry the tears of
those who weep.
Hear us, Lord.

You wept at the grave of Lazarus, your friend; comfort us
in our sorrow.
Hear us, Lord.

You raised the dead to life; give to our brother (sister)
eternal life.
Hear us, Lord.

You promised paradise to the thief who repented; bring
our brother (sister) to the joys of heaven.
Hear us, Lord.

Our brother (sister) was washed in Baptism and anointed
with the Holy Spirit; give *him* fellowship with all your
saints.
Hear us, Lord.

He was nourished with your Body and Blood; grant *him* a
place at the table in your heavenly kingdom.
Hear us, Lord.

72   *Burial of the Dead: Rite Two*

Comfort us in our sorrows at the death of our brother
(sister); let our faith be our consolation, and eternal life
our hope.

Silence may be kept.

*The Celebrant concludes with one of the following or some other
prayer*

Lord Jesus Christ, we commend to you our brother (sister)
N., who was reborn by water and the Spirit in Holy
Baptism. Grant that *his* death may recall to us your victory
over death, and be an occasion for us to renew our trust
in your Father's love. Give us, we pray, the faith to follow
where you have led the way; and where you live and
reign with the Father and the Holy Spirit, to the ages of
ages. *Amen.*

or this

Father of all, we pray to you for *N.*, and for all those
whom we love but see no longer. Grant to them eternal
rest. Let light perpetual shine upon them. May *his* soul
and the souls of all the departed, through the mercy of God,
rest in peace. *Amen.*

*When there is no Communion, the service continues with the
Commendation, or with the Committal.*

At the Eucharist

The service continues with the Peace and the Offertory on page 81.

*Unless the Committal follows immediately in the church, the following
Commendation is used, but if the body is not present, the service
continues with the [blessing and] dismissal on page 86.*

The Commendation

The Celebrant and other ministers take their places at the body.
This anthem, or some other suitable anthem, or a hymn, may be sung
or said

Give rest, O Christ, to your servant(s) with your saints,
where sorrow and pain are no more,
neither sighing, but life everlasting.

You only are immortal, the creator and maker of mankind;
and we are mortal, formed of the earth, and to earth
shall we return. For so did you ordain when you created
me, saying, "You are dust, and to dust you shall return."
All of us go down to the dust; yet even at the grave we
make our song: Alleluia, alleluia, alleluia.

Give rest, O Christ, to your servant(s) with your saints,
where sorrow and pain are no more,
neither sighing, but life everlasting.

The Celebrant, facing the body, says

Into your hands, O merciful Savior, we commend your
servant *N.* Acknowledge, we humbly beseech you, a sheep
of your own fold, a lamb of your own flock, a sinner
of your own redeeming. Receive *him* into the arms of your
mercy, into the blessed rest of everlasting peace, and into
the glorious company of the saints in light. *Amen.*

The Celebrant, or the Bishop if present, may then bless the people,
and a Deacon or other Minister may dismiss them, saying

Let us go forth in the name of Christ.
Thanks be to God.

As the body is borne from the church, a hymn, or one or more of these anthems may be sung or said

Christ is risen from the dead, trampling down death by death, and giving life to those in the tomb.

The Sun of Righteousness is gloriously risen, giving light to those who sat in darkness and in the shadow of death.

The Lord will guide our feet into the way of peace, having taken away the sin of the world.

Christ will open the kingdom of heaven to all who believe in his Name, saying, Come, O blessed of my Father; inherit the kingdom prepared for you.

Into paradise may the angels lead you. At your coming may the martyrs receive you, and bring you into the holy city Jerusalem.

or one of these Canticles,

The Song of Zechariah, *Benedictus*
The Song of Simeon, *Nunc dimittis*
Christ our Passover, *Pascha nostrum*

The Committal

p 501

The following anthem or one of those on pages 51-52 is sung or said

Everyone the Father gives to me will come to me;
I will never turn away anyone who believes in me.

He who raised Jesus Christ from the dead
will also give new life to our mortal bodies
through his indwelling Spirit.

My heart, therefore, is glad, and my spirit rejoices;
my body also shall rest in hope.

You will show me the path of life;
in your presence there is fullness of joy,
and in your right hand are pleasures for evermore.

Then, while earth is cast upon the coffin, the Celebrant says these words

In sure and certain hope of the resurrection to eternal life through our Lord Jesus Christ, we commend to Almighty God our *brother N.*, and we commit *his* body to the ground;* earth to earth, ashes to ashes, dust to dust. The Lord bless *him* and keep *him*, the Lord make his face to shine upon *him* and be gracious to *him*, the Lord lift up his countenance upon *him* and give *him* peace. *Amen.*

*Or the deep, *or* the elements, *or* its resting place.

The Celebrant says

The Lord be with you.
People   And also with you.
Celebrant Let us pray.

Celebrant and People

Our Father, who art in heaven,	Our Father in heaven,
hallowed be thy Name,	hallowed be your Name,
thy kingdom come,	your kingdom come,
thy will be done,	your will be done,
on earth as it is in heaven.	on earth as in heaven.
Give us this day our daily bread.	Give us today our daily bread.
And forgive us our trespasses,	Forgive us our sins
as we forgive those	as we forgive those
who trespass against us.	who sin against us.

And lead us not into temptation, Save us from the time of trial,
  but deliver us from evil.   and deliver us from evil.
For thine is the kingdom, For the kingdom, the power,
  and the power, and the glory,   and the glory are yours,
  for ever and ever. Amen.   now and for ever. Amen.

Other prayers may be added.

Then may be said

p. 502

Rest eternal grant to *him*, O Lord;
And let light perpetual shine upon him.

May *his* soul, and the souls of all the departed,
through the mercy of God, rest in peace. *Amen.*

The Celebrant dismisses the people with these words

    Alleluia. Christ is risen.
People   The Lord is risen indeed. Alleluia.
Celebrant Let us go forth in the name of Christ.
People   Thanks be to God.

or with the following

The God of peace, who brought again from the dead our
Lord Jesus Christ, the great Shepherd of the sheep, through
the blood of the everlasting covenant: Make you perfect
in every good work to do his will, working in you that
which is well-pleasing in his sight; through Jesus Christ, to
whom be glory for ever and ever. *Amen.*

The Consecration of a Grave

If the grave is in a place that has not previously been set apart for
Christian burial, the Priest may use the following prayer, either before
the service of Committal or at some other convenient time

O God, whose blessed Son was laid in a sepulcher in the garden: Bless, we pray, this grave, and grant that *he* whose body is (is to be) buried here may dwell with Christ in paradise, and may come to your heavenly kingdom; through your Son Jesus Christ our Lord. *Amen.*

Additional Prayers

Almighty God, with whom still live the spirits of those who die in the Lord, and with whom the souls of the faithful are in joy and felicity: We give you heartfelt thanks for the good examples of all your servants, who, having finished their course in faith, now find rest and refreshment. May we, with all who have died in the true faith of your holy Name, have perfect fulfillment and bliss in your eternal and everlasting glory; through Jesus Christ our Lord. *Amen.*

O God, whose days are without end, and whose mercies cannot be numbered: Make us, we pray, deeply aware of the shortness and uncertainty of human life; and let your Holy Spirit lead us in holiness and righteousness all our days; that, when we shall have served you in our generation, we may be gathered to our ancestors, having the testimony of a good conscience, in the communion of the Catholic Church, in the confidence of a certain faith, in the comfort of a religious and holy hope, in favor with you, our God, and in perfect charity with the world. All this we ask through Jesus Christ our Lord. *Amen.*

O God, the King of saints, we praise and glorify your holy Name for all your servants who have finished their course in your faith and fear: for the blessed Virgin Mary; for the holy patriarchs, prophets, apostles, and martyrs;

and for all your other righteous servants, known to us
and unknown; and we pray that, encouraged by their
examples, aided by their prayers, and strengthened by their
fellowship, we also may be partakers of the inheritance
of the saints in light; through the merits of your Son Jesus
Christ our Lord. *Amen.*

Lord Jesus Christ, by your death you took away the sting
of death: Grant to us your servants so to follow in faith
where you have led the way, that we may at length fall
asleep peacefully in you and wake up in your likeness; for
your tender mercies' sake. *Amen.*

Father of all, we pray to you for those we love, but see no
longer: Grant them your peace; let light perpetual shine
upon them; and, in your loving wisdom and almighty
power, work in them the good purpose of your perfect will;
through Jesus Christ our Lord. *Amen.*

Merciful God, Father of our Lord Jesus Christ who is the
Resurrection and the Life: Raise us, we humbly pray, from
the death of sin to the life of righteousness; that when
we depart this life we may rest in him, and at the resurrection
receive that blessing which your well-beloved Son shall
then pronounce: "Come, you blessed of my Father, receive
the kingdom prepared for you from the beginning of
the world." Grant this, O merciful Father, through Jesus
Christ, our Mediator and Redeemer. *Amen.*

Grant, O Lord, to all who are bereaved the spirit of faith
and courage, that they may have strength to meet the
days to come with steadfastness and patience; not sorrowing
as those without hope, but in thankful remembrance of

your great goodness, and in the joyful expectation of eternal life with those they love. And this we ask in the Name of Jesus Christ our Savior. *Amen.*

Almighty God, Father of mercies and giver of comfort: Deal graciously, we pray, with all who mourn; that, casting all their care on you, they may know the consolation of your love; through Jesus Christ our Lord. *Amen.*

The Holy Eucharist: Rite Two

The Peace

All stand. The Celebrant says to the people

> The peace of the Lord be always with you.
People And also with you.

Then the Ministers and People may greet one another in the name of the Lord.

The Holy Communion

The Celebrant may begin the Offertory with some sentence of Scripture.

Offer to God a sacrifice of thanksgiving, and make good your vows to the Most High. *Psalm 50:14*

During the Offertory, a hymn, psalm, or anthem may be sung.

Representatives of the congregation bring the people's offerings of bread and wine to the deacon or celebrant. The people stand while the offerings are presented and placed on the Altar.

The Great Thanksgiving

Eucharistic Prayer A

The people remain standing. The Celebrant, whether bishop or priest, faces them and sings or says

The Lord be with you.
People And also with you.
Celebrant Lift up your hearts.
People We lift them to the Lord.
Celebrant Let us give thanks to the Lord our God.
People It is right to give him thanks and praise.

Then, facing the Holy Table, the Celebrant proceeds

It is right, and a good and joyful thing, always and everywhere to give thanks to you, Father Almighty, Creator of heaven and earth, through Jesus Christ our Lord; who rose victorious from the dead, and comforts us with the blessed hope of everlasting life. For to your faithful people, O Lord, life is changed, not ended; and when our mortal body lies in death, there is prepared for us a dwelling place eternal in the heavens. Therefore we praise you, joining our voices with Angels and Archangels and with all the company of heaven, who for ever sing this hymn to proclaim the glory of your Name:

Celebrant and People

Holy, holy, holy Lord, God of power and might,
heaven and earth are full of your glory.
  Hosanna in the highest.
Blessed is he who comes in the name of the Lord.
  Hosanna in the highest.

The people stand or kneel.

Then the Celebrant continues

Holy and gracious Father: In your infinite love you made us for yourself; and, when we had fallen into sin and become subject to evil and death, you, in your mercy, sent Jesus Christ, your only and eternal Son, to share our human nature, to live and die as one of us, to reconcile us to you, the God and Father of all.

He stretched out his arms upon the cross, and offered himself, in obedience to your will, a perfect sacrifice for the whole world.

At the following words concerning the bread, the Celebrant is to hold it, or lay a hand upon it; and at the words concerning the cup, to hold or place a hand upon the cup and any other vessel containing wine to be consecrated.

On the night he was handed over to suffering and death, our Lord Jesus Christ took bread; and when he had given thanks to you, he broke it, and gave it to his disciples, and said, "Take, eat: This is my Body, which is given for you. Do this for the remembrance of me."

After supper he took the cup of wine; and when he had given thanks, he gave it to them, and said, "Drink this, all of you: This is my Blood of the new Covenant, which is shed for you and for many for the forgiveness of sins. Whenever you drink it, do this for the remembrance of me."

Therefore we proclaim the mystery of faith:

Celebrant and people

Christ has died.
Christ is risen.
Christ will come again.

We celebrate the memorial of our redemption, O Father, in this sacrifice of praise and thanksgiving. Recalling his death, resurrection, and ascension, we offer you these gifts.

Sanctify them by your Holy Spirit to be for your people the Body and Blood of your Son, the holy food and drink of new and unending life in him. Sanctify us also that we may faithfully receive this holy Sacrament, and serve you in unity, constancy, and peace; and at the last day bring us with all your saints into the joy of your eternal kingdom.

All this we ask through your Son Jesus Christ. By him, and with him, and in him, in the unity of the Holy Spirit all honor and glory is yours, Almighty Father, now and for ever. *AMEN.*

And now, as our Savior Christ has taught us, we are bold to say,	As our Savior Christ has taught us, we now pray,

People and Celebrant

Our Father, who art in heaven, hallowed be thy Name, thy kingdom come, thy will be done, on earth as it is in heaven. Give us this day our daily bread. And forgive us our trespasses, as we forgive those who trespass against us.	Our Father in heaven, hallowed be your Name, your kingdom come, your will be done, on earth as in heaven. Give us today our daily bread. Forgive us our sins as we forgive those who sin against us.

And lead us not into temptation,	Save us from the time of trial,
but deliver us from evil.	and deliver us from evil.
For thine is the kingdom,	For the kingdom, the power,
and the power, and the glory,	and the glory are yours,
for ever and ever. Amen.	now and for ever. Amen.

The Breaking of the Bread

The Celebrant breaks the consecrated Bread.

A period of silence is kept.

Then may be sung or said

[Alleluia.] Christ our Passover is sacrificed for us;
Therefore let us keep the feast. [Alleluia.]

*In Lent, Alleluia is omitted, and may be omitted at other times except
during Easter Season.*

*In place of, or in addition to, the preceding, some other suitable
anthem may be used.*

Facing the people, the Celebrant says the following Invitation

The Gifts of God for the People of God.
and may add Take them in remembrance that Christ died
for you, and feed on him in your hearts by
faith, with thanksgiving.

*The ministers receive the Sacrament in both kinds, and then immediately
deliver it to the people.*

*The Bread and the Cup are given to the communicants with these
words*

The Body (Blood) of our Lord Jesus Christ keep you in
everlasting life. [*Amen.*]

or with these words

The Body of Christ, the bread of heaven. [*Amen.*]
The Blood of Christ, the cup of salvation. [*Amen.*]

During the ministration of Communion, hymns, psalms, or anthems may be sung.

When necessary, the Celebrant consecrates additional bread and wine.

After Communion, the Celebrant says

Let us pray.

Celebrant and People

Almighty God, we thank you that in your great love you have fed us with the spiritual food and drink of the Body and Blood of your Son Jesus Christ, and have given us a foretaste of your heavenly banquet. Grant that this Sacrament may be to us a comfort in affliction, and a pledge of our inheritance in that kingdom where there is no death, neither sorrow nor crying, but the fullness of joy with all your saints; through Jesus Christ our Savior. Amen.

The service continues with the Commendation or Committal, page 74 or 75.

If the body is not present, the service continues with the [blessing and] dismissal.

The Bishop when present, or the Priest, may bless the people.

The Deacon, or the Celebrant, dismisses them with these words

Let us go forth in the name of Christ.
People Thanks be to God.

or this

Deacon Go in peace to love and serve the Lord.
People Thanks be to God.

or this

Deacon Let us go forth into the world,
          rejoicing in the power of the Spirit.
People Thanks be to God.

or this

Deacon Let us bless the Lord.
People Thanks be to God.

*From the Easter Vigil through the Day of Pentecost "Alleluia, alleluia"
may be added to any of the dismissals.*

The People respond Thanks be to God. Alleluia, alleluia.

An Order for Burial

When, for pastoral considerations, neither of the burial rites in this Book is deemed appropriate, the following form is used.

1. The body is received. The celebrant may meet the body and conduct it into the church or chapel, or it may be in place before the congregation assembles.
2. Anthems from Holy Scripture or psalms may be sung or said, or a hymn may be sung.
3. Prayer may be offered for the bereaved.
4. One or more passages of Holy Scripture are read. Psalms, hymns, or anthems may follow the readings. If there is to be a Communion, the last Reading is from the Gospel.
5. A homily may follow the Readings, and the Apostles' Creed may be recited.
6. Prayer, including the Lord's Prayer, is offered for the deceased, for those who mourn, and for the Christian community, remembering the promises of God in Christ about eternal life.
7. The deceased is commended to God, and the body is committed to its resting place. The committal may take place either where the preceding service has been held, or at the graveside.
8. If there is a Communion, it precedes the commendation, and begins with the Peace and Offertory of the Eucharist. Any of the authorized eucharistic prayers may be used.

Note:

The liturgy for the dead is an Easter liturgy. It finds all its meaning in the resurrection. Because Jesus was raised from the dead, we, too, shall be raised.

The liturgy, therefore, is characterized by joy, in the certainty that "neither death, nor life, nor angels, nor principalities, nor things present, nor things to come, nor powers, nor height, nor depth, nor anything else in all creation, will be able to separate us from the love of God in Christ Jesus our Lord."

This joy, however, does not make human grief unchristian. The very love we have for each other in Christ brings deep sorrow when we are parted by death. Jesus himself wept at the grave of his friend. So, while we rejoice that one we love has entered into the nearer presence of our Lord, we sorrow in sympathy with those who mourn.

Additional Material

Opening Sentences

It is of the LORD'S mercies that we are not consumed, because his compassions fail not. They are new every morning: great is thy faithfulness.

For God so loved the world, that he gave his only begotten Son, that whosoever believeth in him should not perish, but have everlasting life.

Verily, verily, I say unto you, He that heareth my word, and believeth on him that sent me, hath everlasting life, and shall not come into condemnation; but is passed from death unto life.

For now we see through a glass, darkly; but then face to face: now I know in part; but then shall I know even as also I am known.

Fight the good fight of faith, lay hold on eternal life, whereunto thou art also called, and hast professed a good profession before many witnesses.

Blessed be the God and Father of our Lord Jesus Christ, which according to his abundant mercy hath begotten us again unto a lively hope by the resurrection of Jesus Christ from the dead, to an inheritance incorruptible and undefiled, and that fadeth not away, reserved in heaven for you.

The righteous live for evermore; their reward also is with the Lord, and the care of them is with the most High. Therefore shall they receive a glorious kingdom, and a beautiful crown from the Lord's hand: for with his right hand shall he cover them, and with his arm shall he protect them.

God is not a God of the dead, but of the living: for all live unto him.

With thee, O Lord, is the fountain of life: in thy light shall we see light.

Jesus said, I am come that they might have life, and that they might have it more abundantly.

Eye hath not seen, nor ear heard, neither have entered into the heart of man, the things which God hath prepared for them that love him.

Jesus said unto him, Verily I say unto thee, Today shalt thou be with me in paradise.

They are before the throne of God, and serve him day and night in his temple: and he that sitteth on the throne shall dwell among them.

Peace I leave with you, my peace I give unto you: not as the world giveth, give I unto you. Let not your heart be troubled, neither let it be afraid.

I would not have you to be ignorant, brethren, concerning them which are asleep, that ye sorrow not, even as others which have no hope. For if we believe that Jesus died and rose again, even so them also which sleep in Jesus will God bring with him.

Let not your heart be troubled: ye believe in God, believe also in me. In my Father's house are many mansions: if it were not so, I would have told you. I go to prepare a place for you. And if I go and prepare a place for you, I will come again, and receive you unto myself; that where I am, there ye may be also.

Blessed are they that mourn: for they shall be comforted.

Be strong and of a good courage, fear not, nor be afraid: for the LORD thy God, he it is that doth go with thee; he will not fail thee, nor forsake thee.

Blessed be God, even the Father of our Lord Jesus Christ, the Father of mercies, and the God of all comfort; who comforteth us in all our tribulation, that we may be able to comfort them which are in any trouble, by the comfort wherewith we ourselves are comforted of God.

For thus saith the LORD, As one whom his mother comforteth, so will I comfort you.

God is our refuge and strength, a very present help in trouble.

Thou wilt keep him in perfect peace, whose mind is stayed on thee: because he trusteth in thee. Trust ye in the LORD for ever: for in the LORD JEHOVAH is everlasting strength.

The eternal God is thy refuge, and underneath are the everlasting arms.

Our help standeth in the Name of the LORD, who hath
made heaven and earth.

For I am persuaded that neither death, nor life, nor angels,
nor principalities, nor powers, nor things present, nor
things to come, nor height, nor depth, nor any other creature,
shall be able to separate us from the love of God, which
is in Christ Jesus our Lord.

I heard a great voice out of heaven, saying, Behold the
tabernacle of God is with men, and he will dwell with
them, and they shall be his people, and God himself shall
be with them, and be their God. And God shall wipe
away all tears from their eyes; and there shall be no more
death, neither sorrow, nor crying, neither shall there be
any more pain: for the former things are passed away.

Psalms

Psalm 39 *Dixi, custodiam*

LORD, let me know mine end, and the number of my days;
    that I may be certified how long I have to live.

Behold, thou hast made my days as it were a span long,
and mine age is even as nothing in respect of thee; *
    and verily every man living is altogether vanity.

For man walketh in a vain shadow,
and disquieteth himself in vain; *
    he heapeth up riches, and cannot tell who shall gather them.

And now, Lord, what is my hope? *
    truly my hope is even in thee.

Deliver me from all mine offenses; *
  and make me not a rebuke unto the foolish.

When thou with rebukes dost chasten man for sin,
thou makest his beauty to consume away, like as it were a
                moth fretting a garment: *
every man therefore is but vanity.

Hear my prayer, O LORD,
and with thine ears consider my calling; *
  hold not thy peace at my tears;

For I am a stranger with thee, and a sojourner, *
  as all my fathers were.

O spare me a little, that I may recover my strength, *
  before I go hence, and be no more seen.

Psalm 84 *Quam dilecta!*

O how amiable are thy dwellings, thou LORD of hosts! *
  My soul hath a desire and longing to enter into the courts
                of the LORD;
  my heart and my flesh rejoice in the living God.

Blessed are they that dwell in thy house; *
  they will be alway praising thee.

Blessed is the man whose strength is in thee; *
  in whose heart are thy ways.

Who going through the vale of misery use it for a well; *
  and the pools are filled with water.

They will go from strength to strength, *
  and unto the God of gods appeareth every one of them
                in Sion.

O LORD God of hosts, hear my prayer; *
  hearken, O God of Jacob.

Behold, O God our defender, *
  and look upon the face of thine anointed.

For one day in thy courts is better than a thousand. *
  I had rather be a door-keeper in the house of my God,
  than to dwell in the tents of ungodliness.

For the LORD God is a light and defense; *
  the LORD will give grace and worship;

And no good thing shall he withhold *
  from them that live a godly life.

O LORD God of hosts, *
  blessed is the man that putteth his trust in thee.

Psalm 91 *Qui habitat*

Whoso dwelleth under the defense of the Most High, *
  shall abide under the shadow of the Almighty.

I will say unto the LORD,
Thou art my hope, and my stronghold; *
  my God, in him will I trust.

For he shall deliver thee from the snare of the hunter, *
  and from the noisome pestilence.

He shall defend thee under his wings,
and thou shalt be safe under his feathers; *
  his faithfulness and truth shall be thy shield and buckler.

Thou shalt not be afraid for any terror by night, *
  nor for the arrow that flieth by day;

For the pestilence that walketh in darkness, *
  nor for the sickness that destroyeth in the noon-day.

A thousand shall fall beside thee,
and ten thousand at thy right hand; *
  but it shall not come nigh thee.

Yea, with thine eyes shalt thou behold, *
  and see the reward of the ungodly.

For thou, LORD, art my hope; *
  thou hast set thine house of defense very high.

There shall no evil happen unto thee, *
  neither shall any plague come nigh thy dwelling.

For he shall give his angels charge over thee, *
  to keep thee in all thy ways.

They shall bear thee in their hands, *
  that thou hurt not thy foot against a stone.

Thou shalt go upon the lion and adder: *
  the young lion and the dragon shalt thou tread under thy feet.

Because he hath set his love upon me,
therefore will I deliver him; *
  I will set him up, because he hath known my Name.

He shall call upon me, and I will hear him; *
  yea, I am with him in trouble;
  I will deliver him, and bring him to honor.

With long life will I satisfy him, *
  and show him my salvation.

Psalm 103 *Benedic, anima mea*

Praise the LORD, O my soul; *
  and all that is within me, praise his holy Name.

Praise the LORD, O my soul, *
  and forget not all his benefits:

Who forgiveth all thy sin, *
  and healeth all thine infirmities;

The LORD is full of compassion and mercy, *
  longsuffering, and of great goodness.

He will not always be chiding; *
  neither keepeth he his anger for ever.

He hath not dealt with us after our sins; *
  nor rewarded us according to our wickednesses.

For look how high the heaven is in comparison of the earth;
  so great is his mercy also toward them that fear him.

Look how wide also the east is from the west; *
  so far hath he set our sins from us.

Yea, like as a father pitieth his own children; *
  even so is the LORD merciful unto them that fear him.

For he knoweth whereof we are made; *
  he remembereth that we are but dust.

The days of man are but as grass; *
  for he flourisheth as a flower of the field.

For as soon as the wind goeth over it, it is gone; *
  and the place thereof shall know it no more.

But the merciful goodness of the LORD endureth for ever
                      and ever upon them that fear him; *
  and his righteousness upon children's children;

Even upon such as keep his covenant, *
  and think upon his commandments to do them.

The LORD hath prepared his seat in heaven, *
   and his kingdom ruleth over all.

O praise the LORD, ye angels of his,
ye that excel in strength; *
   ye that fulfill his commandment, and hearken unto the
              voice of his word.

O praise the LORD, all ye his hosts; *
   ye servants of his that do his pleasure.

O speak good of the LORD, all ye works of his,
in all places of his dominion: *
   praise thou the LORD, O my soul.

Scripture Lessons

Mark 10:13-16

They brought young children to Jesus, that he should
touch them: and his disciples rebuked those that brought
them. But when Jesus saw it, he was much displeased,
and said unto them, Suffer the little children to come unto
me, and forbid them not: for of such is the kingdom of
God. Verily I say unto you, Whosoever shall not receive
the kingdom of God as a little child, he shall not enter
therein. And he took them up in his arms, put his hands
upon them, and blessed them.

Romans 6:3-11

Know ye not, that so many of us as were baptized into
Jesus Christ were baptized into his death? Therefore we are
buried with him by baptism into death: that like as Christ
was raised up from the dead by the glory of the Father,
even so we also should walk in newness of life. For if we
have been planted together in the likeness of his death,
we shall be also in the likeness of his resurrection: knowing
this, that our old man is crucified with him, that the
body of sin might be destroyed, that henceforth we should
not serve sin. For he that is dead is freed from sin. Now
if we be dead with Christ, we believe that we shall also live
with him: knowing that Christ being raised from the dead
dieth no more; death hath no more dominion over him.
For in that he died, he died unto sin once: but in that he
liveth, he liveth unto God. Likewise reckon ye also
yourselves to be dead indeed unto sin, but alive unto God
through Jesus Christ our Lord.

1 Thessalonians 4:13-18

I would not have you to be ignorant, brethren, concerning
them which are asleep, that ye sorrow not, even as others
which have no hope. For if we believe that Jesus died
and rose again, even so them also which sleep in Jesus will
God bring with him. For this we say unto you by the
word of the Lord, that we which are alive and remain unto
the coming of the Lord shall not prevent them which
are asleep. For the Lord himself shall descend from heaven
with a shout, with the voice of the archangel, and with
the trump of God: and the dead in Christ shall rise first:
then we which are alive and remain shall be caught up
together with them in the clouds, to meet the Lord in the
air: and so shall we ever be with the Lord. Wherefore
comfort one another with these words.

Prayers for the Departed

O King of paradise, where light abounds and life reigns:
Give to our dear one who is with thee a full share of
thy treasures, that *he* may always be white with thy purity,
tranquil with thy peace, and glad with thy joy. Let us
live vividly in *his* present love, as *he* lives in ours; until
the time of separation be past, and we are taken to the
place whither *he* has gone before, there to dwell with *him*
in the perfect fellowship that knows no end; through
thy mercy, who, with the Father and the Holy Ghost, dost
live and reign ever, one God, world without end. *Amen.*

We seem to give *him* back to thee, dear God, who gavest
him to us. Yet, as thou didst not lose *him* in giving, so
we have not lost *him* by *his* return. Not as the world
giveth, givest thou, O Lover of souls! What thou givest,
thou takest not away. For what is thine is ours always, if
we are thine. And life is eternal; and love is immortal;
and death is only a horizon; and a horizon is nothing save
the limit of our sight. Lift us up, O God, that we may
see further; cleanse our eyes that we may see more clearly;
draw us closer to thyself, that we may know ourselves
nearer to our beloved who are with thee. And while thy
Son prepareth a place for us, prepare us for that happy
place, that, where they are and thou art, we too may be;
through the same Jesus Christ our Lord. *Amen.*

O God, who knowest the necessities of all thy children:
We pray thee to have in thy holy keeping those precious
souls, nearest and dearest to us, who have departed this life
in thy faith and love. Provide for all their needs, sustain
and comfort them, protect them from all ill, and grant

them eternal joy in thy service. Give them peace and rest in thy Presence, and bring them to that glorious perfection promised to thy saints; for the sake of him who died and rose again for us, thy Son, Jesus Christ our Lord. *Amen.*

O Lord, the God of mercy, unto whom all live: Vouchsafe, we beseech thee, unto this our loved one a place of refreshment, rest, and the light of everlasting glory, where the light of thy Presence shineth for evermore. And grant that finally we may be united with *him* in the joy of thine eternal glory; through Jesus Christ our Lord. *Amen.*

Almighty God, who hast given us the comforting assurance that thou art present in every place to hear the prayers of such as love thee, and to protect those for whom we pray: We commit our dear one to thy favor and care, that *he* may dwell with thee in thy glory, and that we may ever be faithful to *his* memory here on earth, and reunited in communion and fellowship in the life that is to come; through Jesus Christ our Lord. *Amen.*

Grant, O Lord, that the soul of our *brother* departed may rest in thy peace and protection, and reign in thy kingdom in heaven; through the merits and mediation of Jesus Christ, thy Son, our Lord. *Amen.*

O Father, into thy loving hands we entrust the soul of our dear *brother*. Enable us to think of *him* as no farther from us than thy Presence with us, which *he* has helped us to feel very near. And while our minds follow *him* to thy Presence, let a portion of *his* believing, persevering spirit rest upon us, that with *him* we may be of those who, through faith and patience, inherit the promises, and whose lives are hid with Christ in thee. *Amen.*

Defend, O Lord, this thy Child with thy heavenly grace; that *he* may continue thine for ever; and daily increase in thy Holy Spirit more and more, until *he* come unto thy everlasting kingdom. *Amen.*

Almighty God, with whom do live the spirits of just men made perfect: We humbly commend the soul of this thy servant, our dear *brother*, into thy hands, as into the hands of a faithful Creator and most merciful Savior; humbly beseeching thee that *he* may be precious in thy sight. Cleanse *him*, we pray thee, from every stain of sin, that *he* may be presented pure and without spot before thee; through Jesus Christ our Lord. *Amen.*

O God, who bindest us to life by holy and tender ties: We gratefully recall all that our beloved one was to us; all that *he* stood for in the world. May we live even more constantly in the companionship of *his* spirit, and carry out, in the old spheres in which we together moved, so much of *his* purpose as we can. May we be kind to the friends *he* loved; devoted to the community in which *he* lived; loyal to the causes which *he* served. Thus in our life may *he* still live on, to our own comfort, and the welfare of thy world; through Jesus Christ our Lord. *Amen.*

O God, the God of the spirits of all flesh, in whose embrace all creatures live, in whatsoever world or condition they be: We beseech thee for *him* whose name and dwelling-place and every need thou knowest. Lord, vouchsafe *him* light and rest, peace and refreshment, joy and consolation in paradise, in the companionship of saints, in the Presence of Christ, in the ample folds of thy great love. Grant that *his* life may unfold itself in thy sight, and find a sweet employment in the spacious fields of eternity. If *he* hath ever been hurt or maimed by any unhappy word or deed of ours, we pray thee of thy great pity to heal and restore *him*, that *he* may serve thee without hindrance. Tell *him*, O gracious Lord, if it may be, how much we love *him* and miss *him* and long to see *him* again; and if there be ways in which *he* may come, vouchsafe *him* to us as a guide and guard, and grant us a sense of *his* nearness in such degree as thy laws permit. If in aught we can minister to *his* peace, be pleased of thy love to let this be; and mercifully keep us from every act which may deprive us of the sight of *him* as soon as our trial-time is over, or mar the fullness of our joy when the end of the days hath come. Pardon, O gracious Lord and Father, whatsoever is amiss in this our prayer, and let thy will be done; for our will is blind and erring, but thine is able to do exceeding abundantly above all that we ask or think; through the same Jesus Christ our Lord. *Amen.*

We pray thee, O Lord, that thou wilt keep in thy tender love this life which we hold in blessed memory. Help us, who continue here, to serve thee with constancy, trusting in thy promises of eternal life; that hereafter we may be united with thy blessed children in the glory of thy Presence; through Jesus Christ our Lord. *Amen.*

Lord of the living and the dead, infinite Spirit, whose love and goodness we adore: To thee we lift voices of sorrow and of hope. Our hearts are sad because one whom we love has gone from us here. Yet mingled with our grief is gratitude, hope, and trust. As we stand in the presence of our dead, we know that it is not defeat, but victory; that *his* life has not set in a night of gloom, but amid the splendors of thine everlasting day. And we bless and glorify thy holy Name for the grace which thou didst vouchsafe to *him* who has now passed into thy nearer Presence. Help us to know that in thy good time hearts that are sundered here will be reunited in the country of their hopes, where thou wilt make us glad in thine abundant answer to every humble prayer; for the sake of Jesus Christ our Lord. *Amen.*

Father Almighty, God everlasting, Spirit eternal, we bow before thee, for only thy wisdom can know our need and thy compassion measure our sorrow. We do not ask that we may understand the mysteries of life and death, but we pray that thy light may guide us and thy strength sustain us. In thy keeping we trust the spirit of *him* whose earthly work is now ended. *He* asked of thee life, and thou gavest it *him*, even length of days for ever and ever. *He* asked of thee strength, and, by thy gift, *he* has put off that which is mortal and has put on immortality. *He* walked in shadow, and thou hast called *him* into the light of that day which knows no night. Oh how great is thy goodness, which thou hast laid up for them that love thee; which thou hast wrought for them that put their trust in thee! Help us also to walk in trust and to go forward without fear, till the path of life shall bring us to life eternal. We ask it because thy love is from everlasting to everlasting, in Christ Jesus our Lord. *Amen.*

Remember, O God, thy servants and handmaidens who have departed hence in the Lord, especially *N.*, and all others to whom our remembrance is due; give them eternal rest and peace, and to us such a measure of communion with them as thou knowest to be best for us. And bring us all to serve thee in thine eternal kingdom, when thou wilt and as thou wilt, only without shame or sin. Forgive our presumption and accept our prayers, as thou didst the prayers of thine ancient Church; through the same Jesus Christ our Lord. *Amen.*

O God, who art the strength of thy saints, and who redeemest the souls of thy servants: We bless thy Name for all those who have died in the Lord, and now rest from their labors, having received the end of their faith, even the salvation of their souls. Especially we call to remembrance thy loving-kindness and thy tender mercies to this thy servant. For all thy goodness that withheld not *his* portion in the joys of this earthly life, and for thy guiding hand along the way of *his* pilgrimage, we give thee thanks and praise. Especially we bless thee for thy grace that kindled in *his* heart the love of thy dear Name; that enabled *him* to fight the good fight, to endure unto the end, and to obtain the victory; yea, to become more than conqueror, through him that loveth us. We magnify thy holy Name that, *his* trials and temptations being ended, sickness and death being passed, *his* spirit is at home in thy Presence, at whose right hand dwelleth eternal peace. And we beseech thee to grant, O Lord, that we, who rejoice in the triumph of thy saints, may profit by their example, that, becoming followers of their faith and patience, we also may enter with them into an inheritance incorruptible and undefiled, which fadeth not away; through the same Jesus Christ our Lord. *Amen.*

O Father, almighty, all-merciful, all-loving, suffer us not to miss the glory of this hour through yielding to an overwhelming sense of bereavement. Give us eyes to see and hearts to feel the undefeated courage, the invincible faith, the unconquerable love which thou hast revealed to us in this triumphant soul, who has now passed to the reward of those who unfeignedly love thee. Fill our hearts with praise and gratitude for *his* unshaken conviction that no distress, suffering, or perplexity, neither death, nor things present nor things to come, could separate us from the love of God which *he* had seen in Christ Jesus our Lord. Let the light which we beheld in *him* never forsake us. And grant to us *his* faith, *his* courage, *his* hope in any trial which may come to us. Bless us with an ever-abiding sense of *his* presence; and we fervently pray that in us *he* may yet behold the fruitage of the travail of *his* body and soul, and be most gloriously satisfied. And this we ask in the Name of *his* Savior and our Savior, Jesus Christ our Lord. *Amen.*

Almighty God, we entrust all who are dear to us to thy never-failing care and love, for this life and the life to come; knowing that thou art doing for them better things that we can desire or pray for; through Jesus Christ our Lord. *Amen.*

O Almighty God, who hast called us to faith in thee, and hast compassed us about with so great a cloud of witnesses: Grant that we, encouraged by the good examples of thy saints, especially of this thy servant, may persevere in running the race that is set before us, until at length, through thy mercy, we, with them, attain to thine eternal joy; through him who is the author and finisher of our faith, thy Son, Jesus Christ our Lord. *Amen.*

O eternal Lord God, who holdest all souls in life: Give, we beseech thee, to thy whole Church in paradise and on earth thy light and thy peace; and grant that we, following the good examples of those who have served thee here and are now at rest, may at the last enter with them into thine unending joy; through Jesus Christ our Lord, who liveth and reigneth with thee, in the unity of the Holy Spirit, one God, now and for ever. *Amen.*

O God, who art our Father for ever and ever: Bless our beloved who, through the gate of death, have passed into thy nearer Presence. May they be conscious of our love, and we of theirs. In ways we cannot fathom, grant us to help them, even as they are permitted to help us. Give to them such happiness as this world can never know; and, beyond all our power to ask, grant them to be noble and great in thy sight; through Jesus Christ our Lord. *Amen.*

O Lord of love, who art ever close to all thy children: Watch with thy care those dear to us who are now with thee. Be thou about their path; be thou within their hearts; make it their joy to do thy will. Let not distance break the bonds of love that bind us to one another and to thee, but unite us closer in thy love; for the sake of Jesus Christ our Lord. *Amen.*

Look favorably, we humbly beseech thee, O most holy Father, upon the souls of those departed from this world, whose lives here were saddened and darkened, who were embittered and broken and crushed, whose spirits scarcely knew thy grace, through our common neglect and apathy. Restore in them thine image which we have defaced. Lay their sins to our charge, that our common guilt may bring us to repentance and the seeking of thy kingdom on earth; through Jesus Christ our Lord. *Amen.*

O God, the Creator and Disposer of life: To all who have gone to their rest in the faith of Christ, grant those good things which thou hast prepared for those who love thee, which eye hath not seen, nor ear heard, neither hath entered into the heart of man to conceive; and for those departed this life in ignorance or defiance of thee, we would plead the intercession of him who in the agony of crucifixion could cry: Father, forgive them, for they know not what they do; even the same thy Son, our Savior Jesus Christ. *Amen.*

Have mercy, O Lord, upon the souls of the faithful departed. Give them eternal rest, let light perpetual shine upon them, and may they rest in peace; through Jesus Christ our Savior. *Amen.*

O God, the Maker and Redeemer of all believers: Grant to the souls of the faithful departed the unsearchable benefits of thy Son's passion; that, in the day of his appearing, they may be manifested as thy children; through the same Jesus Christ our Lord. *Amen.*

O Lord, by whom all souls do live: We thank thee for those who, following in the steps of thy dear Son, have entered into the place whither he went before to prepare for them. We trust them to thy care; and we pray thee that, by thy grace, we may be brought to enjoy with them the endless life of glory; through the same Jesus Christ our Lord. *Amen.*

We commend unto thee, O Lord, all those who have departed this life in the spirit of tranquillity and trustfulness; that, having put their hope in thee, they may pass through the valley of the shadow in peace, and may enter into the rest that remaineth for the people of God; through our Savior Jesus Christ. *Amen.*

Almighty, everliving God, the Source of all being and life, whose mercies are infinite and whose love is unceasing: To thee we commend all souls departed, praying thee to cleanse them from every taint and trace of sin, that, in the communion of thy saints, they may find the joy and peace of a perfect life; through the all-sufficient merits of our only Redeemer, Jesus Christ. *Amen.*

O thou, who hast ordered this wondrous world, who knowest all things in heaven and earth: So fill our hearts with trust in thee, that, by night and by day, at all times and in all seasons, we may without fear commit those who are dear to us to thy never-failing love, for this life and for the life to come; through Jesus Christ our Lord. *Amen.*

O thou, who art the God of the generations of men: We thank thee for all who have walked humbly with thee, and especially for those near to us and dear, in whose lives we have seen a vision of thy beauty. May we know that in the body or out of the body they are with thee. Make us glad in their living; comfort and teach us through their dying. Unite us still, God of our souls, in one household of faith and love, one family in heaven and upon earth, to serve the Lord Christ, who liveth and reigneth with thee and the Holy Ghost, one God, world without end. *Amen.*

We thank thee, O God, for all the goodness and courage which have passed from the life of this thy servant into the life of others, and have left the world richer for *his* presence —for a life's task faithfully and honorably discharged; for good humor and gracious affection and kindly generosity; for sadness met without surrender, and weakness endured without defeat; through Jesus Christ our Lord. *Amen.*

Before thee, O heavenly Father, we remember *him* who
has passed from our midst into the fuller light of thine
eternal Presence. We thank thee for *his* loyalty to duty
and *his* love of the good, and for all those noble qualities
of mind and soul that endeared *him* to us. May we have
the assurance of *his* continued fellowship in thee, and realize
that there is no separation between those that love, even
though converse and communion be no longer possible
according to the flesh. Hear, O God our Father, the prayers
that follow our beloved one upon *his* unseen way, and
grant that both we and *he*, in every condition thy wisdom
ordains, may grow and continue in the knowledge of
thee which alone is eternal life; through Jesus Christ our
Lord. *Amen.*

O God, from whose love neither space nor time can separate
us: We thank thee that those who are absent from us
are still present with thee. We trust them to thy loving
care, knowing that underneath are thine everlasting arms;
and beseeching thee to grant that both they and we,
drawing nearer unto thee, may be drawn nearer to one
another; through Jesus Christ our Lord. *Amen.*

As we bless thy holy Name, O Lord, for thy servants who
have departed this life in thy faith and love, so we beseech
thee to give us grace to follow their good examples, and
to carry on the work which they began. Grant, O Lord, we
pray thee, that the offering of their lives may not have
been made in vain; that we and all thy people may hear the
call to nobler living, which sounds in our ears from the
graves of those who have died that we might live; that we
may dedicate our lives anew to the work of bringing in
thy kingdom upon earth; that so, out of years of sin
and misery and loss, there may arise a better nation and a
better world; through Jesus Christ our Lord. *Amen.*

Father, we thank thee for the faithful souls that have blessed the world, whose lives shine as the light; holy ones who have feared God, who have bravely upheld the right, and generously lived for others' good; who have freely chosen suffering rather than sin, and felt thy favor to be better than life. Oh may their pure and noble lives animate and quicken our hearts; and in our souls may there burn a desire like them to become true children of God; through Jesus Christ our Lord. *Amen.*

We thank thee, O God, for this thy servant patient in tribulation; rejoicing in hope; continuing instant in prayer; not slothful in business; given to hospitality. Having fought the good fight and kept the faith, grant to *him*, we beseech thee, the crown of life that fadeth not away; through Jesus Christ our Lord. *Amen.*

Master divine, we bless thee that those who rest in thee, who have passed forward from this world's twilight into the full noontide glory of thy Presence, have evermore immortal youth in thee. We thank thee that with their frail flesh they have laid by for ever the weakness and weariness, the despondency and the gloom, wherewith this human flesh doth overshadow the undying spirit, and the toils and snares whereby we in this world are enmeshed. We thank thee that they have put on immortal joy, immortal freshness of spirit, immortal and unquenchable love, poured forth freely for ever. We thank thee also that we may share with them in their eternal youth, their eternal joy, putting on morning by morning the fresh robes of thy life within our souls; who, with the Father and the Holy Ghost, dost live and reign one God, for ever and ever. *Amen.*

O God of all the living, we thank thee for the happy memory of those who have gone from this transitory life into the eternal joy of thy Presence. Thine they were upon the earth, as we are thine; and thine are they and we in differing experience still. Though our eyes cannot see them and our ears no longer hear their remembered voices, we bless thee that they are never absent from thy loving care. We thank thee for their lives of earthly service, for the happy days we spent in their companionship, for the example of their faith and patience, and for the teaching of their words and deeds. We confess to thee our neglect and transgressions, our coldness and misapprehension while they lived upon the earth, which we may no more confess to them. But our hearts have rest, knowing that thy love changeth not, and that they see thy face with unobstructed vision. Help us so to live that they may welcome us with joy when at last we come to thee; through Jesus Christ our Lord. *Amen.*

We thank thee, O Lord, for the dear and faithful dead, for those who have made the distant heavens a home for us, and whose truth and beauty are even now in our hearts. One by one thou dost gather the scattered families out of the earthly life into the heavenly glory, from the distractions and strife and weariness of time to the peace of eternity. We thank thee for the labors and joys of these mortal years. We thank thee for the deep sense of the mysteries that lie beyond our dust, and for the eye of faith, which thou hast opened for all who believe in thy Son, to outlook that mark. May we live altogether in thy faith and love, and in that hope which is full of immortality; through the same Jesus Christ our Savior. *Amen.*

O thou Lord of all worlds, we bless thy Name for all those who have entered into their rest, and reached the promised land where thou art seen face to face. Give us grace to follow in their footsteps, as they followed in the footsteps of thy holy Son. Encourage our wavering hearts by their example, and help us to see in them the memorials of thy redeeming grace, and pledges of thy heavenly might in which the weak are made strong. Keep alive in us the memory of those dear to ourselves who have passed from this world, and make it powerful to subdue within us every vile and unworthy thought. Grant that every remembrance, which turns our hearts from things seen to things unseen, may lead us always upward unto thee, till we too come to the eternal rest which thou hast prepared for thy people; through the same Jesus Christ our Lord. *Amen.*

Almighty God, we offer unto thee most high praise and hearty thanks for the wonderful grace and virtue which thou hast manifested in all thy saints, and in all other holy persons upon earth, who by their lives and labors have shone forth as lights in the several generations of the world; such as were the holy prophets, apostles, and martyrs, whom we remember with honor and commemorate with joy; and for whom, as also for all other thy happy servants, our fathers and brethren, who have departed this life with the seal of faith, we praise and magnify thy holy Name; most humbly desiring that we may still continue in that holy communion, and enjoy the comfort thereof, following, with a glad will and mind, their holy examples of godly living and steadfastness in thy faith; through Jesus Christ our Lord. *Amen.*

Be mindful, O Lord, of the souls of thy servants and handmaidens who have gone before us with the sign of faith, especially of this thy servant. To *him,* and to all who rest in Christ, mercifully grant a place of refreshment, light, and peace; through the same Jesus Christ our Savior. *Amen.*

O God, whose love embraceth thy whole family in heaven and earth: Grant that this thy servant, having laid aside the garment of mortality, may enter more and more into thy Presence, and find therein the fullness of thy joy; through Jesus Christ our Lord. *Amen.*[1]

O God, who declarest thine almighty power chiefly in showing mercy and pity: Receive the supplications and prayers which we offer before thee for the soul of thy departed servant; and, forasmuch as in this mortal life *he* put *his* trust in thee, vouchsafe *him* now a place in the glory of thy Presence; through Jesus Christ our Lord, who with thee in the unity of the Holy Spirit liveth and reigneth ever, one God, world without end. *Amen.*

We thank thee, O God, for the saints of all the ages; for those who in times of darkness kept the lamp of faith burning; for the great souls who saw visions of larger truth and dared to declare it; for the multitude of quiet and gracious souls whose presence has purified and sanctified the world; and for those known and loved by us, who have passed from this earthly fellowship into the fuller light of life with thee; through Jesus Christ our Lord. *Amen.*

Almighty God, whose love is over all thy works in this and every world: Into thy hands we commit the soul of this loved one whom thou hast taken into the world of light; beseeching thee to grant *him* the unutterable joys of thine eternal kingdom, and unto all who mourn *him* strength to abide thy will in fortitude and patient faith; through Jesus Christ our Lord. *Amen.*

O God, with whom dwell the spirits of just men made perfect: We praise thee for the upright, the brave, the believing of all generations, for those who by word or work or life have been witnesses of Christ; more especially for those whose memories abide in our hearts, kindred and friends whose faces we behold no more, but whose love is ever with us; the teachers and companions of days gone by, and every soul who has brought us correction, sympathy, and hope, and made thee more real and more dear to us; and we pray thee that we may feel ourselves fellow-citizens with them of the city of God, and kindred in the household of faith; and walking worthily of their high and holy company in the days of our pilgrimage, may find our home with them in thee; through Jesus Christ, their Lord and ours. *Amen.*[2]

Into thy hands, O merciful Savior, we commend the soul of thy servant, now departed from the body. Acknowledge, we humbly beseech thee, a sheep of thine own fold, a lamb of thine own flock, a sinner of thine own redeeming. Receive *him* into the arms of thy mercy, into the blessed rest of everlasting peace, and into the glorious company of the saints in light; where with the Father and the Holy Ghost thou dost live and reign ever, one God, world without end. *Amen.*

O Lord our heavenly Father, we commit to thine unfailing love the beloved soul now departed. We thank thee for the gracious memories which gather about *his* life, for *his* kindly deeds and unselfish thoughts, for the love freely given and the love modestly received; and now at last for quiet release from the burden of the flesh, and entrance into the peace reserved for those who love thee; through Jesus Christ our Lord. *Amen.*

O eternal Father, who dost love us with a greater love than we can either know or understand: We give thee most high praise and hearty thanks for the good example of this thy servant who hath now entered into the larger life of thy heavenly Presence; who here, a tower of strength, stood by us and helped us; who cheered us by *his* sympathy and encouraged us by *his* example; who looked not disdainfully on the outward appearance, but lovingly into the hearts of men; who rejoiced to serve all people; whose loyalty was ever steadfast, and *his* friendship unselfish and secure; whose joy it was to be of service. Grant, we beseech thee, that *he* may find abiding peace in thy heavenly worship, and that we may carry forward his unfinished work for thee on earth; through Jesus Christ our Lord. *Amen.*

We bless thy Name, O Lord, for all who through the ages have sought truth and wrought righteousness and fought the good fight of faith; who being dead live on in the principles and convictions of the world and who themselves are the enriching citizens of thine eternal kingdom. Take the veil from our hearts and join us in one communion with them now and for ever; through him who is the King of saints, Jesus Christ our Lord. *Amen.*[2]

We praise thee, O God, for the prophets and martyrs of humanity, who gave their thoughts and prayers and agonies for thy truth. We praise thee that, amidst the contempt of men, in poverty, loneliness, and imprisonment, thou didst uphold them by thy Spirit. We confess that of these the world was not worthy. Suffer us not, O God, by selfish indifference to forfeit the heritage which we have from them, nor to chill the zeal of any who in the same Spirit strive for the redemption of mankind from ancient error and easy sin; through Jesus Christ our Lord. *Amen.*

Almighty God, we remember before thee this day *him* to whom we are bound in the bond of love; and we pray thee that *he* may ever find *his* fulfillment in the joyful service of thy heavenly kingdom; through Jesus Christ our Lord. *Amen.*

We commend unto thee, O Father, those dear to us from whom we are now separated; and we bless thy Name for our beloved who have been withdrawn from our sight, but are with us always in thee. Teach us to live in the strength of the heritage which they have bequeathed us, and in the power of the endless life which we share with them; through Christ, the Savior and Lord of all. *Amen.*[2]

O Lord Jesus Christ, who hast known on earth the joy and vigor of youth: Grant to *him* whom we love a welcome into thy service, that *he* may share with thee in the abundant life of thine eternal kingdom; where, with the Father and the Holy Ghost, thou reignest God for evermore. *Amen.*

We know, O Lord, as we lay our loved one away, that we give *him* into thy hands, into thy heart; that we give also into thy heart all our love and sorrow, our penitence for whatever more we might have been or done towards *him*, that through thee our thoughts of *him* may reach *him* for ever. We pray thee to forgive us, as we have forgiven each other; to keep alive and true in us our mutual love; and finally to bring us face to face in thy glory, which is thy loving Presence among us all; through Jesus Christ our Savior. *Amen.*

Almighty and everliving God, whose mercies are infinite and whose love is unceasing: We commend unto thee the souls of our dear ones, whose mortal bodies, in times past, have been laid to rest here in hallowed reverence and affection. And we beseech thee that, in thy Presence, they may be united in an eternal fellowship of perfect love; and that finally we may join them in the joy of thy heavenly kingdom, and be partakers of that eternal peace which thou hast promised us; through Jesus Christ our Lord. *Amen.*

O Lord Jesus Christ, who by thy death hast overcome death, and by thy rising to life again hast restored to us everlasting life: Grant to all thy servants who are or shall be buried here, that their bodies may rest in peace; and that through the grave and gate of death they may pass to a joyful resurrection; through thy merits, who livest and reignest with the Father and the Holy Ghost, one God, world without end. *Amen.*

Almighty Father, God of the spirits of all flesh: We bless thy holy Name for all who have completed their earthly course in thy faith and fear, and are now at rest. We remember before thee this day thy servant *N.*, rendering thanks to thee for the gift of *his* friendship, and for *his* life of service and devotion. And in thy loving wisdom and almighty power, work in *him*, we beseech thee, as in us, the good purpose of thy holy will; through Jesus Christ our Savior. *Amen.*

Receive, O Lord, in tranquillity and peace, the souls of thy servants who out of the present life have departed to be with thee. Grant them rest, and place them in the habitations of life, the abodes of blessed spirits; and give them the life that knoweth not age, the good things that pass not away; through Jesus Christ our Lord. *Amen.*

O heavenly Father, help us to trust our loved ones to thy care. When sorrow darkens our lives, help us to look up to thee, remembering the cloud of witnesses by which we are encompassed. And grant that we on earth, rejoicing ever in thy Presence, may share with them the rest and peace which thy Presence gives; through Jesus Christ our Lord. *Amen.*

Almighty God, whose love is over all thy works in this and every world: Into thy hands we commit the souls of loved ones whom thou hast taken into the world of light; beseeching thee to grant unto them the unutterable joys of thine eternal kingdom, and unto all who mourn them strength to abide thy will in fortitude and patient faith; through Jesus Christ our Lord. *Amen.*

Purge the heart and mind and soul of this thy servant, we beseech thee, O Lord, of all that is unworthy of thy Presence, and grant that *he,* being purified of all earthly dross, may be counted worthy to serve thee among thy redeemed; through our Savior Jesus Christ. *Amen.*

Father of all, by whose mercy and grace thy saints remain in everlasting light and peace: We remember with thanksgiving those whom we love but see no longer; and we pray that in them thy perfect will may be fulfilled; through Jesus Christ our Lord. *Amen.*

We thank thee, Lord God, for the grace which thou didst give to those who lived according to thy will, and are now at rest. We pray that their good example may encourage and guide us all the days of our life; through Jesus Christ our Lord. *Amen.*

O God, before whose face the generations rise and pass away, the strength of those who labor, and the repose of the holy and blessed dead: We remember all who have faithfully lived and died, especially *N.* Lift us into light and love, and give us at last our portion with those who have trusted in thee, and striven to do thy will. And unto thy Name, with the Church on earth and the Church in heaven, we ascribe honor and glory, world without end. *Amen.*

Almighty God, we remember this day before thee thy faithful servant *N;* and we pray that, having opened to *him* the gates of larger life, thou wilt receive *him* more and more into thy joyful service, that, with all who have faithfully served thee in the past, *he* may share in the eternal victory of Jesus Christ our Lord; who liveth and reigneth with thee, in the unity of the Holy Spirit, one God, for ever and ever. *Amen.*

Lord of heaven and earth, we pray thee for all thy servants who have entered into the victory of eternal life, whose living was light to our darkness, and whose death, revealing their immortal stature, binds us with powerful and tender ties to heaven and to thee; through Jesus Christ our Lord. *Amen.*

Into thy hands, O God, we commend the souls of all our loved ones (especially *N.*), as into the hands of a faithful Creator and most loving Savior; beseeching thee to grant unto them pardon and peace and, of thine infinite goodness, wisdom and power; and to work in them the good purpose of thy perfect will; through Jesus Christ our Lord. *Amen.*

Help us, O Lord, to know that as we give our loved one into thy hands, we give also into thy heart all our love and sorrow, and our penitence for whatever more we might have done in this earthly life. We pray thee to forgive us, as we have forgiven each other; to keep alive and true in us our mutual love; and finally to bring us face to face with thy glory, thy loving Presence among us all, according to the promise of thy blessed Son, our Savior Jesus Christ. *Amen.*

Unto thee, O Lord, we commend the soul of thy servant departed, that, having died unto the world, *he* may live unto thee: and whatsoever sins *he* hath committed through the frailty of earthly life, we beseech thee to do away by thy most loving and merciful forgiveness; through Jesus Christ our Savior. *Amen.*

Absolve, O Lord, we beseech thee, the soul of this thy servant, that, being dead to the world, *he* may live unto thee; and whatsoever *he* hath done amiss in *his* human manner of life through the frailty of the flesh, do thou wipe away by the pardon of thy merciful goodness; through Jesus Christ our Savior. *Amen.*

Almighty God, we give thee thanks for this thy servant, who, being strong in the Lord and in the power of his might, put on the whole armor of God, that *he* might be able to stand against the wiles of the devil; and, being girt about with truth and having on the breastplate of righteousness and the helmet of salvation, with the shield of faith did quench the fiery darts of the wicked, and with the sword of the Spirit did defeat the enemies of righteousness. Grant, we beseech thee, that now *he* may stand victoriously before thee and continue to serve thee for ever in thy heavenly kingdom; through the same Jesus Christ our Lord. *Amen.*

O God our heavenly Father, we bless thy Name for our comrade in Christ who hath passed through the world making its ways luminous with heavenly glory, and hath entered into that city to which Christ is the unsetting sun. Grant that *he*, continuing to live the truth in love, may grow up into him in all things, which is the Head, even Christ; who with thee and the Holy Ghost liveth and reigneth ever, one God, world without end. *Amen.*

Almighty God, about whose throne ten thousand times ten thousand do continually stand and worship thee: Grant, we beseech thee, that this thy servant, being cleansed from all *his* sins, may come in the unity of the faith and of the knowledge of the Son of God, unto a perfect *man*, unto the measure of the stature of the fullness of Christ, and worship thee among thy saints; through the same Jesus Christ our Lord, who liveth and reigneth with thee and the Holy Ghost, one God, world without end. *Amen.*

O Savior of the world, whose nature and property is ever to have mercy and to forgive, whose will is to have pity on all men, and whose loving-kindness is like the great deep: Stablish, we beseech thee, our loved one, who hath passed from this world of affliction and the shadow of death, in the place where light shineth for ever; in thy mercy, who, with the Father and the Holy Ghost, art one God, world without end. *Amen.*

O God, in whose embrace all creatures live: We beseech thee for *him* whose every need thou knowest. Vouchsafe *him* light and rest, peace and refreshment, joy and happiness in the ample folds of thy great love; through Jesus Christ our Lord. *Amen.*

O loving Lord, whose nature embraceth both fatherhood and motherhood in thy concerned care for all thy children: We commend to thy merciful keeping our dear one who hath entered into the life hereafter. Grant *him* the privilege of knowing what their joy and their glory must be, those endless sabbaths the blessed ones see; through Jesus Christ our Savior. *Amen.*

O Lord God and everlasting Father, who dost in love behold all thy children both here and in paradise: Mercifully receive, we beseech thee, thy servant our comrade, that *he* who hath departed hence in all the vigor and promise of life, may be numbered with those who in thy kingdom find their fulfillment in thy service; through Jesus Christ our Lord. *Amen.*

Prayers for Those in the Armed Services Who Have Died

We remember before thee, O Lord of hosts, all those in the armed forces of our country for whom the trumpets have sounded on the other side. Vouchsafe that, being cleansed from their sins, they may serve thee faithfully in thy heavenly kingdom, as good soldiers under the banner of the Captain of their salvation. May their sacrifices here help to establish the freedom for which they died; and may their good example be a consolation and an encouragement to those who mourn for them. We pray that thy sustaining love may ever surround them, and bring them to the measure of the stature of the fullness of him who fought the good fight and won the victory, thy Son, Jesus Christ our Lord. *Amen.*

O God, whose love is beyond our human understanding, and who hast taught us that none may fall without thy knowledge: Have pity upon all who have fallen in this present conflict; and grant that, by the sacrifice of their lives, they may be brought nigh unto the sacrifice of thy blessed Son, and into closer union with him who gave his life that all might have eternal life, Jesus Christ our Lord. *Amen.*

In remembrance of those who made the great sacrifice, make us better men and women; and give peace in our time, we pray thee, O Lord; through Jesus Christ our Savior. *Amen.*

Remember in thy kingdom, O Lord Christ, those who counted not their lives dear unto themselves, but laid them down for their friends. Shed forth upon them the light of thy countenance; and grant that they may be numbered among the hosts of thy redeemed, going forth conquering and to conquer with thee, their everlasting Lord; who livest and reignest with the Father and the Holy Ghost, one God, world without end. *Amen.*

We commit to thy keeping, O Lord, all those who in our behalf have loved not their lives unto the death. May they bring with them into the heavenly places the memory of a sincere devotion and the joy of a good conscience. And grant unto us here in our warfare that we may hear all the trumpets sounding for them on the other side; through Jesus Christ our Savior. *Amen.*

Almighty God, who hast given unto us the comforting assurance that thou art present in every place to hear the prayers of such as love thee, and to protect those for whom we pray: We commit into thy holy keeping this thy servant who died in the service of *his* country, gratefully

honoring the priceless gift which *he* hath laid upon the
altar of freedom; and beseeching thy continual blessing
upon *him*. Grant that we may not only be faithful to
his memory here on earth, but also to the cause for which
he died; and reunited in communion and fellowship in
the kingdom of thy peace; through Jesus Christ our Lord.
Amen.

Have compassion, O most merciful God, on these thy
servants bereaved and afflicted, and on all who are mourning
for those dear to them. Be thou their Comforter and
Friend, and bring them to a fuller knowledge of thy love.
Assuage the anguish of their bereavement, and leave only
the cherished memory of the loved and lost, and a solemn
pride to have laid so costly a sacrifice upon the altar
of freedom; in the Name of Jesus Christ our Savior. *Amen.*[1]

Almighty God, by whose grace thy people gain courage
through looking unto the heroes of faith: We lift our
hearts in gratitude to thee for all who have lived valiantly
and died bravely that there might be truth, liberty, and
righteousness in our land. Help us to prize highly, and
to guard carefully, the gifts which their loyalty and devotion
have bestowed upon us. Grant us the joy of a living and
vigorous faith, that we may be true as they were true,
loyal as they were loyal, and serve thee and our country
selflessly all the days of our life, and at last receive the
victor's crown; through Jesus Christ our Lord. *Amen.*

Unto thee, O God, be praise and thanksgiving for all those
who have been faithful unto death. Into thy merciful
keeping we commend their souls, beseeching thee to grant
that their love and devotion may bear fruit in us in more
abundant love for others; through him who by his death

hath destroyed death, thy Son, Jesus Christ our Lord. *Amen.*

Almighty God, who didst offer thine only Son to be made perfect through suffering, and to win our salvation by enduring the cross: Sustain with thine uplifting strength all those whose loved ones have given their lives in the service of our country. Redeem, we pray thee, the pain of their bereavement, that, knowing their loss to be the price of our freedom, they may remember the gratitude of the nation for which they gave so costly a sacrifice. And grant, O Lord, that we may highly resolve that these dead shall not have died in vain, but that out of the distress of this present age may arise a new and better world, in which thy will shall be done, and thy Name hallowed; through the same our Savior Jesus Christ. *Amen.*

We commend, O Lord God, into the arms of thy mercy those who have died in their country's service, beseeching for them thy Son's blessing upon all who lay down their life for their friends, and the immortal crown of the faithful who have overcome; through the same Jesus Christ our Lord. *Amen.*

Almighty and everlasting God, in whom all souls live now and evermore, the God not of the dead but of the living: We bless thee for all those who have faithfully lived and died in the service of their country. As we ever hold them in grateful remembrance, do thou in thy love and mercy let light perpetual shine upon them, and bring us all at last into thine eternal kingdom of peace; through Jesus Christ our Savior. *Amen.*

We humbly beseech thee, O Lord of hosts, to accept our thanksgiving for all who have fought a good fight and won the crown of victory, especially for those known to us and dear. Praise be to thee for the memory of their noble example and the inspiration of their high valor and sacrifice. Grant us grace, we pray thee, so to follow them in every gracious virtue of mind and spirit, that with them we may attain at last to thine eternal peace and felicity; through Jesus Christ our Lord. *Amen.*

O eternal God, through whose mighty power our fathers won their liberties of old: We thank thee for all thy servants who have laid down their lives to defend thy gift of freedom. Grant, we beseech thee, that we, and all the people of this land, may be ready to follow their examples of courage and loyalty, and may have grace to maintain our liberties in righteousness and peace; through Jesus Christ our Lord. *Amen.*

Almighty Father, Lord of hosts, we bow in gratitude before thee for this our comrade, as we entrust *him* to thy loving care. We thank thee for *his* friendship, *his* fidelity to duty, and the bravery with which *he* gave the last full measure of devotion. Comfort, we pray thee, *his* loved ones in the hour of their sorrow, and renew in them the courage and steadfastness which come from faith in thee; through Jesus Christ our Lord. *Amen.*

O God, who holdest all souls in life: Receive our humble thanks and hearty praise for all thy servants who have given their lives in the cause of liberty, especially those whom now we silently recall. Blessed be thy glorious Name that thou dost bestow upon them the light of thy Presence, where in the fellowship of faithful people they may win with thee the eternal victory; through our Lord Jesus Christ. *Amen.*

Grant, O Lord, we pray thee, that the offering of this life may not have been in vain; that we and all the people may hear the call to nobler living which sounds in our ears from the graves of those who have died that we might live; and that we dedicate our lives anew to the work of thy kingdom upon earth, that so, out of these years of sin and misery and loss, there may arise a better nation and a fairer world; through Jesus Christ our Savior. *Amen.*

God of our fathers, known of old, Lord of the far-flung battle line: We give thee humble thanks and high praise for the cherished memory and good example of all thy servants who have laid down their lives in the service of our country. We bless thee for their courage and devotion. Accept, we pray thee, their sacrifice, and let it not be in vain that they have died in the cause of righteousness. As they have come out of great tribulation, grant, O Lord, that they may be pardoned and cleansed in the blood of the Lamb, and received into thine everlasting mercy; through Jesus Christ our Savior, to whom with thee and the Holy Ghost, be all honor and glory, world without end. *Amen.*

O Lord our God, whose Name only is excellent, and thy praise above heaven and earth: We give thee hearty thanks for all those who counted not their lives dear unto themselves, but laid them down for their friends; beseeching thee to give them a part and a lot in the good things which thou hast prepared for those whose names are written in the Book of Life. And grant that, having them always in remembrance, we may imitate their faithfulness, and with them inherit the new name which thou hast promised to those who overcome; through Jesus Christ our Lord. *Amen.*

O Lord God Almighty, we give thee most humble thanks for those who have yielded up their lives for the freedom of mankind and in defense of our liberties. Grant, we beseech thee, that their bravery may be remembered, and the people cease not to tell their praise before thee, who gavest the courage, and dost accept the sacrifice; through the Captain of our salvation, Jesus Christ. *Amen.*

We give thee thanks, most mighty Lord, for the life of this happy warrior, who has kept faithful with a singleness of aim, whom every man in arms should wish to be; Grant, we pray thee, that *he* may go gladly on *his* way of service to thee and to others in the life of thy heavenly kingdom; through Jesus Christ our Savior. *Amen.*

We thank thee, O Father, for this thy servant whose warfare is accomplished and whose iniquity is pardoned; and we praise thy Name that *he* hath given to *his* country the service of *his* love, and hath made undaunted the final sacrifice. Grant, we beseech thee, that *he*, having come out of great tribulation, may be meet to dwell with thy faithful soldiers and servants in thy heavenly kingdom, and to rejoice in that blessed country, whose ways are ways of pleasantness, and all whose paths are peace; through him who is the Author and Finisher of our faith, even thy Son, Jesus Christ our Lord. *Amen.*

O God and Father of us all, we praise thee in sincere gratitude for all those who, at their country's call, have met the rude shock of battle, and have surrendered their lives amid the ruthless brutalities of war. Forbid that their suffering and death should be in vain. And we beseech thee, that, through their devotion to duty and suffering, the horrors of war may pass from earth, and that thy kingdom of right and honor, of peace and brotherhood, may be established among men. Comfort, O Lord, all who mourn the loss of those near and dear to them, especially the families of our departed *brothers.* Support them by thy love. Give them faith to look beyond the trials of the present, and to know that neither life nor death can separate us from the love and care of Christ Jesus, in whose Name we pray. *Amen.*

O King eternal, immortal, invisible, who in the righteousness of thy saints hast given us an example of godly life, and in their blessedness a glorious pledge of the hope of our calling: We thank thee for all who have so lived in thy faith and fear, especially those whom we have known and loved, who have passed on into the fuller life in thee; likewise for those who have fallen in battle, whom in honor we remember before thee. And we beseech thee, that, being compassed about with so great a cloud of witnesses, we may also run our race with patience, and with them at the last may receive the crown of glory that fadeth not away; through Jesus Christ our Lord. *Amen.*

Almighty God, our heavenly Father, we commend unto thee the souls of our departed comrades, who gave their lives unselfishly that others might have life, praying that they may continue to serve thee and to rejoice in thine everlasting life. We remember with thankfulness their days with us: their friendship and laughter, their helpfulness and devotion, their courage and strength. We praise thee that their work on earth has been sealed with this sacrifice, and pray that thereby righteousness and freedom, brotherhood and peace may prevail throughout the world; in the Name of him who died on the cross for us all, Jesus Christ our Savior. *Amen.*

Prayers for a Departed Child

O merciful Father, whose face the angels of thy little ones do always behold in heaven: Grant us steadfastly to believe that this thy child hath been taken into the safe keeping of thine eternal love; through Jesus Christ our Lord. *Amen.*

Almighty and merciful Father, who dost grant to children an abundant entrance into thy kingdom: Grant us grace so to conform our lives to their innocency and perfect faith, that at length, united with them, we may stand in thy Presence in fullness of joy; through Jesus Christ our Lord. *Amen.*

O Lord Jesus Christ, who didst take little children into thine arms and bless them: Open thou our eyes, we beseech thee, that we may perceive that this child is in the everlasting arms of thine infinite love, and that thou wilt bestow upon *him* the blessings of thy gracious favor; who livest and reignest with the Father and the Holy Spirit, one God, world without end. *Amen.*

O God, our Father, whose unveiled face the angels of little children do always behold: Comfort and strengthen us in the assurance that what was bound up with our life and made a dear part of our being cannot be lost; that the ties that are broken here are still preserved in the love that made them ours; and that the powers we would have helped to train are now unfolding in the same divine care which inspired our love; through Jesus Christ, thy Son, our Lord. *Amen.*

Our heavenly Father, our hearts are grateful for the joy
which came into our lives from the life of this child while
here on earth. *He* refreshed our souls with *his* smiling
trustfulness, *his* gentleness, and the warmth of *his* love;
and encouraged us to a nobler way of life. May we
all go from strength to strength in our different worlds,
and increase in grace, until at last we are reunited in
thy loving Presence; through Jesus Christ our Lord, who
with thee and the Holy Spirit is one God, world without
end. *Amen.*

O heavenly Father, who hast promised through thy
dearly-beloved Son that the pure in heart shall see thee:
Grant that this thy child may stand ever in thy Presence,
and behold the beauty of thy vision in the joy of thy
service; through the same Jesus Christ our Lord. *Amen.*

O holy Father, whose blessed Son in his love for little
children said, Suffer little children to come unto me, and
forbid them not: We thank thee for this merciful assurance
of thy love, for we believe that thou hast been pleased
to take unto thyself the soul of this thy child who was
dedicated unto thee in baptism. As *he* was a member of
thy suffering kingdom here on earth, so we are certain
that *he* now rejoiceth in thy glorious kingdom in heaven.
Make us as little children in trust and humility, that
by thy grace we may be united both now and hereafter in
thy heavenly love; through the same Jesus Christ our
Lord. *Amen.*

Almighty God, the Father of our Lord Jesus Christ, within
whose arms little children were welcomed, and from
whose lips fell the gracious words that theirs is the kingdom
of heaven: Help us steadfastly to believe that this child,
whom thou didst receive in holy baptism, hath now been

raised above the sorrows and temptations of this present world, to be kept by thee unto everlasting life; and to share with all who by thy mercy serve thee there in the joyful resurrection of the just, and the bliss of the heavenly inheritance; through the same Jesus Christ, thy Son, our Lord. *Amen.*

Heavenly Father, whose face the angels of little children do always behold, and who by thy Son Jesus Christ hast taught us that of such is the kingdom of heaven: We commend unto thy faithful keeping the soul of this little child whom thou hast gathered with the lambs in thy bosom; beseeching thee that thou wilt accept the innocence of this thy little one, cleansing *him* from all stain of earthly life, that *he* may dwell for ever in thy Presence. And this we ask through the same Jesus Christ our Lord. *Amen.*

Our heavenly Father, we thank thee for the blessed ministry of this child who has now gone from our earthly fellowship. *He* has made us glad in his living, and called forth the brightest treasures of our hearts. We rejoice in hope that is full of immortality, and look forward to a happy reunion with *him* in the unseen home of thy love, beyond the mystery where *he* awaits our coming, in the Presence of thy Son, Jesus Christ our Lord. *Amen.*

O merciful God and heavenly Father, of whose kingdom in heaven little children are members, and into which none can enter who becomes not as a little child: We humbly implore thy mercy in behalf of these afflicted parents. Bind up, we pray thee, their broken hearts; comfort them with the blessed assurance that it is well with their loved one; and prepare them for their happy reunion in thine eternal and everlasting glory; through Jesus Christ our Lord. *Amen.*

O God, whose ways are hidden, and yet most wonderful, who makest nothing in vain, and lovest all that thou hast made: Comfort thy servants whose hearts are sore smitten and oppressed; and grant that they may so love and serve thee in this life, that, together with this thy child, they may obtain the fullness of thy promises in the world to come; through Jesus Christ our Lord. *Amen.*

O God, whose most dear Son did take little children into his arms and bless them: Give us grace, we beseech thee, to entrust the soul of this child to thy never-failing care and love, and bring us all to thy heavenly kingdom; through the same thy Son, Jesus Christ, our Lord. *Amen.*

O God, our heavenly Father, who art leading us through the changes of time to the rest and blessedness of eternity: Be thou near to us, as we leave this grave, to comfort and uphold. Make us to know and feel that thy children are precious in thy sight, and that they live evermore with thee, and that thy mercy endureth for ever. We commend to thee these sorrowing parents. Pity them as a father his children; comfort them as a mother her little ones. Touch their wounds with the hands of healing. May strength and consolation be given unto them; may the words of thy Son breathe peace into their troubled hearts. And suffer us not to forget that by the mystery of death we are brought nearer to the Infinite Goodness, in whose bosom we can rest; sure that the God, whom fatherhood and motherhood interpret and reveal, will keep that which we have committed unto him; through the same Jesus Christ our Lord. *Amen.*

Thou gavest *him* into our arms, O Lord, for a little while. Do thou now take *him* into thine arms for ever. It is well with the child. Blessed be God, who in his good time will reunite us in the joy of his Presence; through Jesus Christ our Savior. *Amen.*

Heavenly Father, whose Son our Savior took little children into his arms and blessed them: Receive, we pray thee, thy child N. in thy never-failing care and love, comfort all who have loved *him* on earth; and bring us all to thine, everlasting kingdom; through the same Jesus Christ our Lord. *Amen.*

We give thanks unto thee, O Lord God, heavenly Father, through Jesus Christ, thy dear Son, that thou hast been so graciously present with us in all our needs; and even though the heavy burden of sorrow has come so soon upon us, still thou dost grant us the comforting assurance that all things work together for good to them that love thee. O most merciful Father, we humbly offer thee our love and trust, and tenderly commit the soul of our little one into thy keeping, against the day when we shall be united in thy Presence. And, we beseech thee, take not the comfort of thy Spirit from us, but grant us grace ever to learn and to do thy will; through the same Jesus Christ, thy Son, our Lord. *Amen.*

Prayers for the Bereaved

O merciful Father, who hast taught us in thy holy Word that thou dost not willingly afflict or grieve the children of men: Look with pity, we beseech thee, upon the sorrows of thy *servants* for whom our prayers are offered. Remember *them*, O Lord, in mercy; nourish *their* souls with patience; comfort *them* with a sense of thy goodness; lift up thy countenance upon *them*, and give *them* peace; through Jesus Christ our Lord. *Amen.*

Comfort, O Lord, we pray thee, all who mourn for the loss of those near and dear to them, and look with thy special mercy upon those unable by distance or infirmity to be here today. Be with them in their sorrow; comfort them with a sense of thy Presence, and give them faith to look beyond the troubles of the present time, and to know that neither life nor death can separate them from thy love, which thou hast declared in Christ Jesus our Lord. *Amen.*

Eternal and unchangeable God, in whom alone we can find rest for our weariness and comfort for our sorrow: Keep our hearts, we beseech thee, ever fixed on thee through life and death, waiting patiently for that glorious day when we shall evermore rejoice in the fullness of thy love; through Jesus Christ our Lord. *Amen.*

Our Father in heaven, whose pity is infinite and whose will is sovereign: Be pleased to look upon our sorrow and, for the sake of thy dear Son, lead us through the valley of the shadow into the green pastures of thy loving consolation; that, dwelling with thee in spirit, we may have communion with those we love who are with thee; through the same thy Son, Jesus Christ our Lord. *Amen.*

O heavenly Father, whose blessed Son Jesus Christ did weep at the grave of Lazarus his friend: Look, we beseech thee, with compassion upon those who are now in sorrow and affliction; comfort them, O Lord, with thy gracious consolations; make them to know that all things work together for good to them that love thee; and grant them evermore sure trust and confidence in thy fatherly care; through the same Jesus Christ our Lord. *Amen.*

O heavenly Father, whose unchanging love is sufficient for all our needs: We pray thee to grant the gracious comfort of thy Presence to all who mourn, whose hearts are torn with grief for which no human aid avails; that, even in the desolation of their loss, they may feel the calm assurance of thy mercy, and know the blessing of thy peace which passeth understanding; through Jesus Christ our Lord. *Amen.*

Our Father in heaven, whose pity is infinite and whose will is sovereign: We beseech thee, in thy merciful love, to look upon our sorrow, and enable us so to hear thy holy Word, that, through patience and comfort of the Scriptures, we may have hope; and to send to us the Holy Ghost the Comforter, promised by thy dear Son, that he may strengthen and console us; through the same Jesus Christ our Lord. *Amen.*

Lord Jesus, we beseech thee, by the loneliness of thy suffering on the cross, be nigh unto all them that are desolate and in sorrow today; and let thy Presence transform their loneliness into comfort, consolation, and holy fellowship with thee, who art with the Father and the Holy Ghost, one God, world without end. *Amen.*

Almighty and everlasting God, the Comfort of the sad, and the Strength of sufferers: Let the prayers of those that cry out of any tribulation come unto thee; that all may rejoice to find that thy love and mercy are present with them in their afflictions; through Jesus Christ our Lord. *Amen.*

Almighty God, who in the time of our shadow and darkness canst be our only true and lasting light: Look upon us, thy sad children, we humbly beseech thee, with thy constant mercy, and give us the spirit of understanding promised by thy dear Son. When our eyes no longer behold those whom we love, and we listen for the footsteps of those who have passed from our sight, and hear them not; enable us to turn to thee. When our hearts fail us, and we sigh for that which cannot be, and no traveller comes back from that bourne, and there is none to comfort us; grant us still to trust in thee. And give us the comfort of Christ through the Spirit of truth, we pray thee; for the sake of the same Jesus Christ our Lord. *Amen.*

O Lord, our heavenly Father, who orderest all things for our eternal good: Mercifully enlighten our minds, and give us a firm and abiding trust in thy love and care. Silence our murmurings, quiet our fears, and dispel our doubts, that, rising above our afflictions and sorrows, we may come to the fuller knowledge of thy love, and rest in thee, the Rock of everlasting strength; through Jesus Christ our Savior. *Amen.*

O Lord, by all thy dealings with us, whether of joy or pain, of light or darkness, let us be brought to thee. Let us value no treatment of thy grace simply because it makes us happy or because it makes us sad, because it gives us or denies us what we want; but may all that happens to us bring us closer unto thee; that, knowing thy perfectness, we may be sure that in every disappointment thou art still loving us, and in every darkness thou art still enlightening us, and in every enforced idleness thou art still using us, and in every death thou art still giving us life, as in his death thou didst give life to thy Son, our Savior Jesus Christ. *Amen.*

O Almighty God, who art found of those who seek thee in loneliness, and whose portion is sufficient for the sorrowful soul: Pour out, we pray thee, thy blessing upon these thy servants, bereaved and afflicted. Let not thy grace of patience fail them, nor thy love forsake them; but do thou so comfort and sustain their hearts, that in the land of peace and rest, when the time cometh, they too may find an everlasting home. Grant this, we beseech thee, for his sake who hath gone thither to prepare a place for us, thy Son, our Savior Jesus Christ. *Amen.*

O blessed Jesus, who thyself didst weep by the grave of Lazarus, and knowest all human sorrows: Do not blame our tears, but bind up the wounds of our stricken hearts. Bless to us this season of sorrow. Through the deep mysteries of pain may we pass to closer communion with thee and with one another. One more link is loosed which bound us to earth; may it now bind us to heaven. And grant that hereafter, with *him* who has passed within the veil, we may dwell with thee in glory everlasting; who, with the Father and the Holy Ghost, art one God, world without end. *Amen.*

Comfort us, we beseech thee, gracious God, whensoever we are cast down and faint of heart amidst the sorrows and difficulties of this world. And grant that, by the energy of thy Holy Spirit, we may be enabled to go on our way rejoicing, and at length appear before thee in the city where the vision of thy peace is revealed; through thy Son, our Savior Jesus Christ. *Amen.*

O Lord, we pray thee to keep our souls from the temptations of this hour of mourning, that we may neither sorrow as those without hope, nor lose our trust in thee; but that

the darker this earthly scene becomes, the lighter may
be our vision of that eternal world where all live unto thee.
Grant to us who are still upon earth to be steadfast in
faith, joyful in hope, and rooted in love, so that at the last
we may be reunited with them in the land of everlasting
life; through Jesus Christ our Lord. *Amen.*

Blessed Jesus, who hast borne our griefs and carried our
sorrows: Satisfy us with thy mercy, and strengthen us
with thy might; that, in all our sorrow and desolation, we
may find peace in thy Presence, and comfort in thy love;
who art our Hope and our Strength, our very present Help
in trouble. *Amen.*

O thou, who art the God of all comfort, who healest the
broken in heart and bindest up their wounds: Mercifully
look upon those who are at this time bereaved. Be near
them in their sorrow, and let their sorrow draw them
nearer unto thee. Now that earthly joys and comfort fail,
may the things unseen and eternal grow more real, more
present, more full of meaning and power. Let thy strength
sustain their weakness; thy grace free their sorrow from
bitterness; and thy peace fill their minds with perfect
trust in thee; through Jesus Christ our Savior. *Amen.*

O heavenly Father, who understandest all thy children:
Through thy gift of faith may we bring our perplexities to the
light of thy wisdom, and receive the blessed encouragement
of thy sympathy, and a clearer knowledge of thy will;
through Jesus Christ our Lord. *Amen.*

Father of mercies and God of all comfort, look in pity, we
pray thee, on these thy servants whose joy has been
turned into sorrow, whose house has been left unto them
desolate. They have drunk of the cup of bitterness; do

thou give unto them the cup of consolation. Let not their faith die, nor their light go out in darkness. Comfort them with the assurance that their loved one is with thee, and will be remembered in the day when thou makest up the number of thy saints. In this hour of trial draw them close to thy love, and help them to trust in thee, and to believe that deeper than the pain and the mystery of death are the everlasting arms of thy tender mercy; through Jesus Christ our Lord. *Amen.*

We bless thee, O Lord, for those great spirits through all the ages, who, in deepest misfortune, discovered thee and were laid hold of by thee; who, when sorrow lowered most heavily and life's meaning was most inscrutable, in that hour felt most surely beneath them the strength of the everlasting arms; who fought a dark way through the valley of the shadow of death into a glorious victory of faith, where they feared no evil, because thou wert with them; and who went forth from days of sadness, with gladness in their souls and a song of triumph in their hearts, to take up once more life's unfinished course. Grant a portion of their spirit to those who this day bow in sorrow and grief; and do thou be the Comforter of their souls; through Jesus Christ our Lord. *Amen.*

O God, in the hour of death we turn in faith to thee, who art the Author of eternal life. Strengthen us, we beseech thee, with the knowledge that beyond the vicissitudes of the flesh lie the realities of the spirit. Send us thy light that we may see the hidden depths of thy love; and grant us comfort in the unseen things which are eternal; through Jesus Christ our Lord. *Amen.*

Our Father in heaven, who art always near to all thy
children, yet never nearer than in the time of their sorrow:
Make thyself known here to those who mourn, we pray
thee, in thy consoling love and supporting strength; and
keep them ever close to thee, that they may be close
to their dear one who is with thee. And we beseech thee
for *him* whom we commend into thy loving care; that *he*,
being cleansed from all *his* sins, may go from strength
to strength in the life of perfect service in thy heavenly
kingdom. Fill *his* life with thy joy and peace; and let light
perpetual shine upon *him*; through him who is the Light
of the world, thy Son, Jesus Christ our Lord. *Amen.*

O God of all consolation, comfort all those who have lost
their dear ones, and strengthen them with the knowledge
of thy love. Help them to know thee, the Giver of life,
as their Friend; and to remember that there is no separation
in the realm of love; through Jesus Christ our Lord. *Amen.*

O God our Father Almighty, whose faithfulness never
faileth: Comfort, we pray thee, all who mourn the loss of
this thy servant; that they may abide patiently upon thee,
and know that neither height nor depth, nor things present
nor things to come, nor death nor life, can separate thy
children from thy love, which is in Christ Jesus our Lord.
Amen.

Heavenly Father, to whom all our sorrows are known:
Grant to us in our loss and loneliness the comfort of thy
grace. We thank thee for the love that has been ours
and that even now is ours, since we are still one in thee.
Give us day by day strength to bear bravely our burden,
and unto our life's end help us to live in the light of the
world to come; through Jesus Christ our Lord. *Amen.*

God of all comfort, tenderly uphold these thy servants
who in this home and family feel most keenly the loss
of their dear one's immediate presence. Make them glad in
the remembrance of *his* love and affection, and grateful
that *he* was spared to see *his* children grown into *manhood
and womanhood*. And while our minds follow *him* to
thy Presence, let a portion of *his* persevering spirit rest
upon us, and finally, we pray thee, bring us face to face in
thy glory, which is thy loving Presence amongst us all;
through thy Son Jesus Christ our Lord. *Amen.*

O God, the Author of all true and tender affections: Behold
our grief, whose depth is the measure of a love which
was thy gift. Out of the deep we call upon thy Name, for
there is mercy with thee, and in thy Word is our trust.
Save us, O Father, even while the waves of sorrow engulf
us. Help us to entrust to thine eternal keeping the deathless
love which binds us to one whose going from our sight
makes our heart faint within us. Steady us to hold with
tranquil hand the candle of faith, a flame undying amid the
changes and chances of our mortality. So shall we permit
thee to guide our steps along the hard path which lies
before us, and which, if we are true, will reveal itself as
the highway of the King who reigneth over heaven and
earth, our Savior Jesus Christ. *Amen.*[1]

Almighty God, who hast taught us that they who mourn
shall be comforted: Grant that in all our grief we may
turn to thee; and, because our need is beyond the help of
men, grant us the peace of thy consolation and the joy
of thy love; through Jesus Christ our Lord. *Amen.*

Almighty God, whose Son our Lord Jesus Christ won the
victory over death: Grant that all who mourn the loss

of those dear to them may enter into his victory, and find comfort, hope, and peace in him, who is the resurrection and the life, the same thy Son, Jesus Christ our Lord. *Amen.*

O Lord Jesus Christ, who didst have compassion upon the widow of Nain and say unto her, Weep not; and by thine apostle hast bidden us not to be sorry as men without hope for them that sleep in thee: Visit, we beseech thee, with thy compassion those who mourn the loss of their beloved, and when thou comest into thy kingdom, wipe away all tears from their eyes; who livest and reignest with the Father and the Holy Spirit ever, one God, world without end. *Amen.*

In thy boundless compassion, O Lord, console all who mourn. Give to them that faith which sees in death but the gate of life eternal, so that with quietude and fearlessness they may continue their course on earth, until by thy call they are united to their loved ones gone before; through Jesus Christ our Lord. *Amen.*

O God, thou Helper of the helpless: Sustain and comfort every mourning heart. In the knowledge that in thy holy keeping are the living and the dead, give us strength to return to the quiet duties of our place. With chastened desires, with better aspirations, with truer diligence, with less trust in ourselves and more rest in thee, may we dedicate ourselves anew to the service of thy will; that, in the faith and spirit of him who was made perfect through suffering, we may henceforth live our lives; through the same Jesus Christ our Lord. *Amen.*

Have compassion, O Lord, upon all who are mourning for those dear to them, and upon all who are lonely and desolate. Be thou their Comforter and Friend; give them such earthly help and consolation as thou seest to be best for them; and grant them a fuller knowledge and realization of thy love; for thy holy Name's sake. *Amen.*

O eternal Father, who didst not spare thine only Son, but gavest him to be the Redeemer of mankind: Draw near, we beseech thee, to those who mourn the loss of loved ones. Comfort them in their loneliness; supply all their need; suffer them never to doubt thy love, but draw them through their sorrow into closer fellowship with thee; through the same Jesus Christ our Lord. *Amen.*

Jesus, Lord of life and Conqueror of death, who didst dry the tears of the widow of Nain: Look with compassion on those who grieve for the loss of one dear to them. Make them to know that thou art with them even in the darkest hours; and in thy Presence may they find courage, comfort, and peace; for thy love's sake. *Amen.*

Lord Christ, who didst speak words of comfort to thy friends Martha and Mary in their hour of sorrow: Give consolation and courage to those who mourn today, and may they find their peace and hope in thee, the Resurrection and the Life; for thy tender mercies' sake. *Amen.*

Heavenly Father, our refuge and strength in every time of need: Help and comfort us today. Increase our faith, dispel our fears, revive our hope; and lift us from the darkness of our grief to the light of thy Presence; through Jesus Christ our Lord. *Amen.*

O Lord Jesus Christ, who wept at the grave of Lazarus:
We commend to thy tender care and compassion those
whose loss is greatest at this time, because their lives were
closest and their love was strongest. In the midst of their
deep sorrow give them the comfort of thy Presence,
and the courage and faith which they need to face life again
in the days to come. And may thy peace be with them,
O Lord, both now and always. *Amen.*

Prayers for the Congregation

To thee, the everlasting Father, before whom stand the
spirits of the living and the dead, we offer hearty thanks
for all the fair and noble memories of those whom we
have known and loved, for all who have witnessed a good
confession for the faith, for all who have laid down their
lives for their friends, for all the unknown dead whose
forgotten labors have made earth better for their presence:
humbly beseeching thee that we may live worthily, as
becometh those who are bought with a great price; that we
may hereafter meet them unashamed in thy Presence;
through Jesus Christ our Lord. *Amen.*

O God, who hast prepared for those who love thee such
good things as pass man's understanding: Pour into our
hearts such love toward thee, that we, loving thee above
all things, may obtain thy promises, which exceed all
that we can desire; through Jesus Christ our Lord. *Amen.*

Almighty and merciful God, of whose only gift it cometh that thy faithful people do unto thee true and laudable service: Grant, we beseech thee, that we may so faithfully serve thee in this life, that we fail not finally to attain thy heavenly promises; through the merits of Jesus Christ our Lord. *Amen.*

O most loving Father, who willest us to give thanks for all things, to dread nothing but the loss of thee, and to cast all our care on thee, who carest for us: Preserve us from faithless fears and worldly anxieties, and grant that no clouds of this mortal life may hide from us the light of that love which is immortal, and which thou hast manifested unto us in thy Son, Jesus Christ our Lord. *Amen.*

We beseech thee, O Lord, pour thy grace into our hearts; that, as we have known the incarnation of thy Son Jesus Christ by the message of an angel, so by his cross and passion we may be brought unto the glory of his resurrection; through the same Jesus Christ our Lord. *Amen.*

Almighty and everlasting God, who, of thy tender love towards mankind, hast sent thy Son, our Savior Jesus Christ, to take upon him our flesh, and to suffer death upon the cross, that all mankind should follow the example of his great humility: Mercifully grant, that we may both follow the example of his patience, and also be made partakers of his resurrection; through the same Jesus Christ our Lord. *Amen.*

Grant, O Lord, that as we are baptized into the death of thy blessed Son, our Savior Jesus Christ, so by continual mortifying our corrupt affections we may be buried with him; and that through the grave, and gate of death, we may pass to our joyful resurrection; for his merits, who died, and was buried, and rose again for us, the same thy Son Jesus Christ our Lord. *Amen.*

Almighty God, who through thine only-begotten Son Jesus Christ hast overcome death, and opened unto us the gate of everlasting life: We humbly beseech thee that, as by thy special anticipating grace thou dost put into our minds good desires, so by thy continual help we may bring the same to good effect; through the same Jesus Christ our Lord, who liveth and reigneth with thee and the Holy Ghost ever, one God, world without end. *Amen.*

Grant, we beseech thee, Almighty God, that like as we do believe thy only-begotten Son our Lord Jesus Christ to have ascended into the heavens; so we may also in heart and mind thither ascend, and with him continually dwell, who liveth and reigneth with thee and the Holy Ghost, one God, world without end. *Amen.*

O God, the King of glory, who hast exalted thine only Son Jesus Christ with great triumph unto thy kingdom in heaven: We beseech thee, leave us not comfortless; but send to us thine Holy Ghost to comfort us, and exalt us unto the same place whither our Savior Christ is gone before, who liveth and reigneth with thee and the same Holy Ghost, one God, world without end. *Amen.*

O Almighty God, who hast knit together thine elect in one communion and fellowship, in the mystical body of thy Son Christ our Lord: Grant us grace so to follow thy blessed Saints in all virtuous and godly living, that we may come to those unspeakable joys which thou hast prepared for those who unfeignedly love thee; through the same thy Son Jesus Christ our Lord. *Amen.*

O King eternal, immortal, invisible, who in the righteousness of thy saints hast given us an example of godly life, and in their blessedness a glorious pledge of the hope of our calling: We beseech thee that, being compassed about with so great a cloud of witnesses, we may run with patience the race that is set before us, and with them receive the crown of glory that fadeth not away; through Jesus Christ our Lord. *Amen.*

O thou, who art heroic Love: Kindle, we pray thee, in our hearts that high spirit of adventure, in which men scorn the way of safety and seek danger in order to do thy will. Help us to prove worthy of their brave and loving company, who, at thy bidding, put everything upon the hazard, until they passed over, and all the trumpets sounded for them on the other side. *Amen.*

Almighty and everlasting God, who dost enkindle the flame of thy love in the hearts of the Saints: Grant to us, thy humble servants, the same faith and power of love; that, as we rejoice in their triumphs, we may profit by their examples; through Jesus Christ our Lord. *Amen.*

Grant, O Lord, that, keeping in glad remembrance those who have gone before, who have stood by us and helped us, who have cheered us by their sympathy and strengthened us by their example, we may seize every opportunity of life, and rejoice in the promise of a glorious resurrection with them; through Jesus Christ our Savior. *Amen.*

Through the day long support us, O God, till the evening time, when comes thy stillness in the rising stars, and our work is done. Then bring us to our resting place, where we may wait thy waking at the dawn; through Christ our Lord. *Amen.*

O Lord Jesus Christ, who didst reveal thyself more fully to thy disciples after thou wast taken from them: Grant us faith to believe that no separation of time or place can sever thy servants from their eternal union in thee; who art with the Father and the Holy Ghost, one God, world without end. *Amen.*

O heavenly Father, who in thy Son Jesus Christ hast given unto us a true faith and a sure hope: Help us, we pray thee, amidst all the things that pass our understanding, to live as those who believe and trust in thy fatherly care, in the communion of saints, the forgiveness of sins, and the resurrection to life everlasting; and strengthen, we beseech thee, this faith and hope in us all the days of our life; through the love of the same thy Son, our Savior Jesus Christ. *Amen.*

O thou, in whom we live and move and have our being, who seest where we are blind, who knowest where we are ignorant: Be with us at this time, and grant unto us faith and hope and love without measure. O thou Good Shepherd of thy sheep, lead us through our sorrow and trouble to thy heavenly fold, where peace and joy for ever dwell, and where thou art all in all; for thy Name's sake. *Amen.*

Our heavenly Father, we rejoice in the blessed communion of all thy saints, wherein thou givest us also to have a part. We remember before thee all who have departed this life in thy faith and love, and especially those most dear to us. We thank thee for our present fellowship with them, for our common hope, and for the promise of future joy. Let the cloud of witnesses, the innumerable company of those who have gone before and entered into rest, be to us an example of godly life. And even now may we be refreshed with their joy, that so with patience we may run the race that remains before us, looking unto Jesus, the Author and Finisher of our faith; and finally obtain an entrance into thine everlasting kingdom, the glorious assembly of the saints, and with them ever worship and adore thy glorious Name, world without end. *Amen.*

O God, who art the Comfort of them that mourn, the Repose of them that triumph: We rejoice in the communion of thy saints. We remember before thee all who have faithfully lived, all who have peacefully passed into thy nearer Presence, especially those most dear to us. May we have the assurance of their continued fellowship in thee, and realize that, though converse be no longer possible according to the flesh, there is no separation in the realm of love, where the Church on earth is one with the Church in heaven; in Jesus Christ our Lord. *Amen.*

Grant us, O God, the assurance that in the grasp of thy love all is utterly safe; that our souls may commit unto thee our life, and those who are dearer by far than our life, with certainty, unflinching and absolute, that in thy home, with thee, to thine own children, never through all eternity, can harm befall, because of Jesus Christ our Lord. *Amen.*

O Lord of life, who dwellest in eternity, and who hast planted in our hearts the faith and hope which look beyond our mortal life to another, even a heavenly country: We give thanks to thee this day for the bright shining of the light of immortality in Jesus Christ. As he hath showed us the blessedness of heaven on earth, and hath called us into a kingdom not of this world, so may our life be made ever richer in the things that do not pass away. Raise us up, we pray thee, in the power of his Spirit, from the death of sin to the life of righteousness. Prepare us to follow him, in hope and trust, through all the darkness of the grave into the world of light whither he hath led the way. And when our spirits shrink before the mysteries of life and death, may we be comforted by the thought of that immortal love which knoweth no change, and feel that, whether we live or die, we are safe in thine everlasting arms; through the same Jesus Christ our Lord. *Amen.*

Weak are we all and dying, O God; give us thy peace, strength for life's battle while it lasts, and rest at the close of day when work is done. Keep us beneath the shadow of thy great protection, till, o'er the hills of time, the angels of thy glory sing again; through Christ our Lord. *Amen.*

O Lord God, grant to each and all of us, so to be true to our high calling here on earth, that when we, each in his appointed time, shall be summoned to join the great company of departed souls, we may pass hence in peace and without fear, looking humbly for that fuller light which shall break upon us when the morning is come upon the unseen shore. Grant this, O Lord, for his sake, who is our life, and in whose Presence is the fullness of joy, Jesus Christ our Lord. *Amen.*

Father and King, we thank thee that in thyself all spiritual values are for ever conserved; that nothing true, noble, and pure in action or in character can for one moment of all eternity be lost; but that all such things, being of thine eternal nature, for ever are treasured and perfected in thyself. We thank thee that though these our bodies, these poor vehicles of thy self-expression in human goodness, beauty, and truth, must of necessity fail and be scattered in dust, yet the souls that have so shown forth thyself live for ever, perfected and rejoicing, in thee. We thank thee for this clear assurance of immortality in the incarnation of thine own nature of love within human flesh. We thank thee that our souls are given us to be thy expression on earth, and the perpetual sharers of thy blissful communion in heaven, where with our beloved we shall rejoice in thee for ever, O thou Life of our souls; through Jesus Christ our Lord. *Amen.*

Grant us, heavenly Father, above all things that can be desired, to rest in thee; and in thee to have our hearts at peace. Thou art the true peace of the soul, thou its only rest; for thou hast made us for thyself, and our hearts are restless until they rest in thee; through Jesus Christ our Lord. *Amen.*

O Lord, we pray thee, give us of thy strength, that we may live more bravely and faithfully for the sake of those who are no longer with us here on earth. And grant us so to serve thee, day by day, that we may find eternal fellowship with them; through him who died and rose again for us all, thy Son, Jesus Christ our Lord. *Amen.*

Lord, we would learn to trust in thee at all times. We think we are trusting thee when the sunlight falls unbroken and bright upon our way; but when the clouds gather and the storm breaks, often our hearts faint and our faith loses its vision. May we have such faith as will feel thy Presence in the dark, and walk calmly through the storm. We would learn, when we are sorrowful and downcast, to be still and know that thou art God. May we cease our struggling and worrying, and let thy way prevail with us; until around our restlessness flows thy rest, to renew our vigor to fight the good fight of faith, and to win the victory; through Jesus Christ our Savior. *Amen.*

O everlasting God, in whom we live and move and have our being: We bow in deepest reverence before thee, the Lord of life and death. We know not when our earthly life shall end, our fleeting days be numbered; but in our ignorance and helplessness we cast ourselves upon thy merciful forgiveness. Awaken in our hearts, we pray thee, the consciousness of thine eternity which bounds our mortal life, and teach us so to live and trust in thee that we may not fear to die. And this we ask in the Name of Jesus Christ, our everliving Lord and Savior. *Amen.*

Our Father, unto thee, in the light of our Savior's blessed life, we would lift our souls. We thank thee for that true Light shining in our world with still-increasing brightness. We thank thee for all who have walked therein, and especially for those near to us and dear, in whose lives we have seen this excellent glory and beauty. May we know that in the body or out of the body they are with thee, and that when these earthly days come to an end, it is not that our service of thee and of one another may cease, but that it may begin anew. Make us glad in all who have faithfully lived and nobly died. Lift us into light and love and purity and blessedness, and give us at last our portion with those who have trusted in thee, and sought, in small things as in great, in things temporal and in things eternal, to do thy holy will; through the same Jesus Christ our Lord. *Amen.*

O God, the protector of all that trust in thee, without whom nothing is strong, nothing is holy: Increase and multiply upon us thy mercy; that, thou being our ruler and guide, we may so pass through things temporal, that we finally lose not the things eternal. Grant this, O heavenly Father, for the sake of Jesus Christ our Lord. *Amen.*

O God, who on the mount didst reveal to chosen witnesses thine only-begotten Son wonderfully transfigured, in raiment white and glistering: Mercifully grant that we, being delivered from the disquietude of this world, may be permitted to behold the King in his beauty, who with thee, O Father, and thee, O Holy Ghost, liveth and reigneth, one God, world without end. *Amen.*

O Lord our God, from whom neither life nor death can separate those who trust in thy love, and whose love holds in its embrace thy children in this world and in the next: So unite us to thyself, that in fellowship with thee we may always be united to our loved ones, whether here or there; give us courage, constancy, and hope; through him who died and was buried and rose again for us, thy Son, Jesus Christ our Lord. *Amen.*

We give thee thanks, O Lord, for lives at rest, for every heart that loved righteousness and every mind that looked to things of others, and every soul that walked humbly with thee, for whom heaven has opened to receive new riches in their characters, who now dwell with the saints in light. Grant that we may be followers of their work of faith and labor of love in patience and in hope, and enter with them into thy purposes for the earth here, and thus be at home with them and thee for ever; through Jesus Christ our Savior. *Amen.*

O Lord our Shepherd and Guide, grant us to walk through the valley of the shadow of death, fearing no evil, lacking nothing, accompanied by thee, who thyself hast passed that way, and made it light; and now livest and reignest in the glory of the eternal Trinity, world without end. *Amen.*

Unite us, O God, in one communion with all the saints, with the souls of the righteous, and with the spirits of just men made perfect in thy Presence. We remember all who have faithfully lived, all who have peacefully died; especially those near to us and dear. Grant that, being compassed about with so great a cloud of witnesses, we may run with patience the race that is set before us, looking unto him who is the Author and Finisher of our Faith, Jesus Christ our Lord. *Amen.*

Eternal Father, the dwelling-place of thy children in all generations, before whom stand the spirits of the living and the dead: We thank thee for the heritage of them that fear thy Name and for the noble succession of the faithful in which thou hast set us; for all who throughout the ages have done justly, loved mercy, and walked humbly with thee; and for the wise of every land who have led mankind into truth. More especially we bless thee for the Gospel of thy grace in Jesus Christ; for the apostles who have spread it throughout the earth; for martyrs who have testified their faith by their blood; for scholars who have interpreted it to the mind of successive generations; for pastors and leaders of thy Church who have counselled young and old in the way of Christ; and for countless men and women, learned and simple, in whom his Spirit has lived and wrought throughout the centuries. And we remember those through whom he came to us, the guides of our childhood and the inspiration of our later years, comrades in the service of thy kingdom who, being dead, yet speak to us; beseeching thee to keep us loyal to the trust which they have committed to us, to enable us to pass it on with increase to them who shall come after, and to grant us enriching communion with them in thee, both now amid earth's shadows, and for ever in that life where they see eye to eye and know as they are known; through the same Jesus Christ our Lord. *Amen.* [2]

O God, who in the multitude of thy saints hast compassed us about with so great a cloud of witnesses: Grant us so to run the race that is set before us, that, rejoicing in their fellowship, we may at length receive the crown of life which thy Son hath promised to them that win the victory; through the same Jesus Christ our Lord. *Amen.* [1]

Grant us, O Lord, the peace of claiming thee in death as our Father, because we have served thee in life as our God; for the sake of Jesus Christ our Savior. *Amen.*

O God, who hast brought us near to an innumerable company of angels, and to the spirits of just men made perfect: Grant us during our earthly pilgrimage to abide in their fellowship, and in thy heavenly country to become partakers of their joy; through Jesus Christ our Lord. *Amen.*

Almighty God, who by thy Son Jesus Christ hast brought life and immortality to light, and hast taught us in thy holy Word to regard death not as the end, but as a new beginning, beyond which lie life and love, thought and labor, bliss and joy: We bless thy holy Name for this thy revelation, humbly beseeching thee that we may show forth our thankfulness for the same, not only with our lips, but in our lives, by yielding ourselves wholly to thy service, and by walking before thee all our days with that serenity and righteousness which befit the heirs of eternal life; through the same Jesus Christ our Lord. *Amen.*

Eternal God, before whom stand the living and the dead: We praise thy Name for ten thousand times ten thousand in the world unseen, whose faith lives on in our souls, whose knowledge lights our path, whose tasks have fallen to our hands; and especially for friends whose faces we see no more, but whose love is with us always. Grant that, as we hold them in grateful remembrance, the sanctity of their goodness may hallow our earthly days, and devote us to diligent labor and trustful patience, until thou bring us with them to the company of the saints in light; through Jesus Christ, their Lord and ours. *Amen.*[2]

Father of our spirits, from whom we come and unto whom we go, and from whose love in Christ Jesus our Lord neither death nor life nor things present nor things to come nor height nor depth can separate us: Thou art our dwelling-place in all generations. We thank thee for all who have faithfully lived and peacefully died, for all enriching memories and uplifting hopes, for the sacred and tender ties that bind us to the unseen world, for the dear and holy dead who encompass us like a cloud of witnesses and make the distant heaven the home of our hearts. Make us followers of those who through faith and patience now inherit the promises; through the same Jesus Christ our Lord. *Amen.*[2]

O heavenly Father, help us to trust our loved ones to thy care. When sorrow darkens our lives, help us to look up to thee, remembering the cloud of witnesses by which we are encompassed. And grant that we on earth, rejoicing ever in thy Presence, may share with them the rest and peace which thy Presence gives; through Jesus Christ our Lord. *Amen.*

Lord God of the hopeful, we bless thy Name for those in every generation who have lived with their faces towards the sunrise, who have refused to be content with things as they were, who have possessed the love which believeth and hopeth all things and never faileth, whose eager eyes have welcomed each new ray of light here, and been gladdened by the daybreak yonder, and still look for the glorious light of the perfect day when thy glory shall be revealed, and all flesh shall see it together. Inspire us with their expectancy, and make us both to labor for, and to depend confidently on thee to grant us, those things for which we pray, with the trust of Jesus Christ. *Amen.*[2]

Grant us, Almighty God, thy peace that passeth understanding, that amid the sorrows and troubles of this our life we may rest in thee; knowing that all things are in thee, not beneath thine eye only, but under thy care, governed by thy will, guarded by thy love, so that with a quiet heart we may meet the storms of life, the cloud and the thick darkness, rejoicing to know that the darkness and the light are both alike to thee. Guide, guard, govern us this day; through Jesus Christ our Lord. *Amen.*[2]

Grant, O God, that the experiences of death may quicken
in us a new fidelity to life. So ennoble and uplift us,
that here we may worthily pass our days, and finally enter
thy heavenly gates with clean hands and a pure heart;
through Jesus Christ our Lord. *Amen.*

O God, who holdest all souls in life: Cleanse our sorrow
by thy gift of faith, and confirm in our hearts the knowledge
of him who is the Resurrection and the Life, thy Son, Jesus
Christ our Lord. *Amen.*[1]

O King of saints, who hast not entered into thy triumph
alone but attended by ten thousand times ten thousand:
We bless thee for those whom we have known and loved.
Let their presence on the heights draw us upwards as
we toil and struggle; let their victory make us of good
courage; let their faith and patience be our inspiration and
our power; and by thy grace may we too some day stand
above all that today tempts and soils and casts us down,
and in the heavenly places find our eternal home; where
with the Father and the Holy Ghost, thou dwellest for
evermore. *Amen.*[2]

We bless thy Name, O Lord, for the faithful of all the ages
who shone as lights in their several generations, and now
dwell with thee in that city to which Christ is the unsetting
sun. And we beseech thee, keep us one in faith with
thy Church on earth, one in hope with thy saints in heaven,
and one in love with thy children everywhere; through
the same Jesus Christ, the Savior and Lord of all. *Amen.*[2]

Teach us, O Lord, to live as those prepared to die. When
the summons comes, soon or late, teach us to die as those

prepared to live; that, living or dying, we may be with thee, and that nothing henceforward, either in life or in death, shall be able to separate us from thy love, which is in Christ Jesus our Lord. *Amen.*

Grant, we beseech thee, most merciful Lord, that we may live in simple trust that thou art ever doing that which is best for all thy children, and that our beloved will find perfect fulfillment in thy glorious and loving Presence; through our Redeemer, Jesus Christ. *Amen.*

O Lord our God, from whom neither life nor death can separate those who trust in thy love, and whose love holds in its embrace thy children in this world and in the next: So unite us to thyself, that in fellowship with thee we may be always united to our loved ones whether here or there; give us courage, constancy, and hope; through him who died and was buried and rose again for us, Jesus Christ our Lord. *Amen.*

Grant, O Lord, that they, who here lay the bodies of their departed to rest in the hope of the resurrection to eternal life, may evermore steadfastly believe and continue in the communion of saints; through Jesus Christ our Savior. *Amen.*

Most merciful Father, who hast been pleased to take unto thyself the soul of this thy servant (*or* this thy child): Grant to us who are still in our pilgrimage, and who walk as yet by faith, that, having served thee with constancy on earth, we may be joined hereafter with thy blessed saints in glory everlasting; through Jesus Christ our Lord. *Amen.*

Bring us, O Lord God, at our last awakening into the house and gate of heaven; to enter into that gate and dwell in that house, where there shall be no darkness nor dazzling, but one equal light; no noise nor silence, but one equal music; no fears nor hopes, but one equal possession; no foes nor friends, but one equal identity; no ends nor beginnings, but one equal eternity, in the habitations of thy majesty and of thy glory, world without end. *Amen.*

We thank thee, O Lord our God, that the life which we now live in Christ is part of the life which is eternal, and the fellowship which we have in him unites us with thy whole Church on earth and in heaven; and we pray that, as we journey through the years, we may know joys which are without end, and at last come to the abiding city, where thou dost reign for evermore. *Amen.*

Almighty God, Lord of life and Vanquisher of death: We praise thee for the sure and certain hope of eternal life, which thou hast given us in the resurrection of our Lord Jesus Christ; and we pray that all who mourn the loss of those dear to them may enter into his victory and know his peace; for his Name's sake. *Amen.*

Grant unto us, O God, to trust thee not for ourselves alone, but for those also whom we love, and are hid from us by the shadow of death; that, as we believe thy power to have raised our Lord Jesus Christ from the dead, so we may trust thy love to give eternal life to all who believe in him; through the same Jesus Christ our Lord. *Amen.*

O Almighty God, who alone canst order the unruly wills and affections of sinful men: Grant unto thy people, that they may love the thing which thou commandest, and desire that which thou dost promise; that so, among the sundry and

manifold changes of the world, our hearts may surely there
be fixed, where true joys are to be found; through Jesus
Christ our Lord. *Amen.*

O God, from whom no secrets are hid: We confess to thee
our resentment at our loneliness, now that our beloved
has passed from our sight; and our frustration that we cannot
command the world in accordance with our own wishes.
Grant us the humility to know that all things work together
for good to them that love thee; that thy loving Presence
is ever with us to comfort and uphold; and that when we are
with thee, we are also with our beloved who are with thee,
in Jesus Christ our Lord. *Amen.*

Eternal God, our heavenly Father, who lovest us with an
everlasting love, and canst turn the shadow of death into
the morning: Help us now to wait upon thee with reverent
and submissive hearts. In the silence of this hour speak to us
of eternal things, that through patience and comfort of
the scriptures we may have hope, and be lifted above our
darkness and distress into the light and peace of thy Presence;
through Jesus Christ our Lord. *Amen.*

Lord, we pray thee that thou wilt open our eyes to behold
the heaven that lies about us, wherein they walk who,
being born to the new life, serve thee with the clearer
vision and the greater joy; through Jesus Christ our Savior.
Amen.

O Lord, support us all the day long of this troublous life,
until the shadows lengthen, and the evening comes, and
the busy world is hushed, and the fever of life is over,
and our work is done. Then, in thy great mercy, grant us
a safe lodging, and a holy rest, and peace at the last;
through Jesus Christ. *Amen.*

God of all grace, who didst send thy Son our Savior Jesus
Christ to bring life and immortality to light: Most humbly
and heartily we give thee thanks that by his death he
destroyed the power of death, and by his glorious resurrection
opened the kingdom of heaven to all believers. Grant us
assuredly to know that because he lives, we shall live also;
and that neither death nor life, nor things present nor things
to come, shall be able to separate us from thy love, which
is in the same Jesus Christ our Lord. *Amen.*

Almighty God, who hast given us grace at this time with one
accord to make our common supplications unto thee; and
dost promise that, when two or three are gathered together
in thy Name, thou wilt grant their requests: Fulfill now,
O Lord, our desires and petitions for thy departed servant,
as may be most expedient for *him*; granting us in this world
knowledge of thy love, and in the world to come life
everlasting. *Amen.*

Almighty God, our loving Father, we confess to thee at
this time our feelings of guilt and anger and vexation
at the death of this thy servant; our sense of not having
done all that we should for *his* welfare; our selfishness in
placing our own pleasure before *his* needs. Make us truly
penitent; forgive us our sins, and with *him* bring us all
to everlasting life; through him who died that we might be
forgiven, thy Son, Jesus Christ our Lord. *Amen.*

O God, whose mighty power brings good out of evil and
life out of death: Grant us a patient faith in time of darkness,
and enlighten our understanding with the knowledge
of thy ways; through Jesus Christ our Lord. *Amen.*

Grant us, Lord, the wisdom and the grace to use aright the time that is left to us here on earth. Lead us to repent of our sins, the evil which we have done and the good which we have not done; and strengthen us to follow the steps of thy Son, in the way that leadeth to the fullness of eternal life; through the same Jesus Christ our Savior. *Amen.*

Almighty God, grant that we, with all those who have believed in thee, may be united in the full knowledge of thy love, and the unclouded vision of thy glory; through Jesus Christ our Lord. *Amen.*

We give thee thanks, O Lord Christ, that the life which we now live in thee is part of the life which is eternal, and the fellowship which we have with thee unites us with our brethren both on earth and in heaven. Grant that, as we journey through the years, we may know joys which are without end, and at the last come to that abiding city, where thou livest and reignest with the Father and the Holy Spirit, one God, world without end. *Amen.*

Grant, we beseech thee, Almighty God, that, being compassed about by so great a cloud of witnesses, we may run with patience the race that is set before us, looking unto Jesus the author and finisher of our faith; so that, this life ended, we may be gathered with those whom we have loved into the kingdom of thy glory, where there shall be no more death, neither sorrow nor sighing, neither shall there be any more pain, for the former things have passed away; through him who maketh all things new, even the same Jesus Christ our Lord. *Amen.*

Eternal God and Father, whose love is stronger than death:
We rejoice that the dead as well as the living are in thy
love and care; and as we remember with thanksgiving
those who have gone before us in the way of Christ, we
pray that we may be counted worthy to share with them
the life of thy kingdom; through the same Jesus Christ
our Lord. *Amen.*

Grant, O Lord, that we may ever walk in thy Presence,
with thy love in our hearts, thy truth in our minds,
thy strength in our wills; that, when we finally stand before
thee, it may be with the assurance of thy welcome and
the joy of our homecoming; through our Savior Jesus Christ.
Amen.

May God in his infinite love and mercy bring the whole
Church, living and departed in the Lord Jesus, to a joyful
resurrection and the fulfillment of his eternal kingdom,
through the power of the Holy Spirit. *Amen.*

O Almighty God, the God of the spirits of all flesh:
Multiply, we beseech thee, to those who rest in Jesus, the
manifold blessings of thy love, that the good work which
thou didst begin in them may be perfected unto the day
of Jesus Christ. And of thy mercy, O heavenly Father,
vouchsafe that we, who now serve thee here on earth, may
at the last, together with them, be found meet to be
partakers of the inheritance of the saints in light; for the
sake of the same thy Son, Jesus Christ, our Lord and
Savior. *Amen.*

Committals

Unto Almighty God we commend the soul of our *brother* departed, and we commit *his* body to the ground; earth to earth, ashes to ashes, dust to dust; in sure and certain hope of the Resurrection unto eternal life, through our Lord Jesus Christ; at whose coming in glorious majesty to judge the world, the earth and the sea shall give up their dead; and the corruptible bodies of those who sleep in him shall be changed, and made like unto his own glorious body; according to the mighty working whereby he is able to subdue all things unto himself.

We commend into thy hands, most merciful Father, the soul of our *brother* departed, and we commit *his* body to the ground; earth to earth, ashes to ashes, dust to dust; in sure and certain hope of the life of the world to come; through our Lord Jesus Christ, who shall fashion anew our earthly body, that it may be like unto his own glorious body, according to the mighty working whereby he is able to subdue all things unto himself.

Unto Almighty God we commend the soul of our *brother* departed, and we commit *his* body to the ground; earth to earth, ashes to ashes, dust to dust; in firm and abiding faith that, as *he* hath borne the image of the earthy, so also *he* doth now bear the image of the heavenly. The dust returns to the earth as it was, but the spirit hath returned unto God who gave it.

Unto Almighty God we commend the soul of our *brother* departed, and we commit *his* body to the ground; earth to earth, ashes to ashes, dust to dust; in firm and abiding faith that *his* soul, clothed anew with a spiritual body, lives for ever; and praying that, through God's great mercy, *he* may attain at last unto the measure of the stature of the fullness of Christ.

Forasmuch as the spirit of our *brother* departed hath entered into life immortal, we commit *his* body to its resting place; and *his* spirit we commend unto God, even as Jesus said upon the cross, Father, into thy hands I commend my spirit.

We commend into thine eternal and everlasting keeping, most merciful Father, the soul of our *brother* departed, and we commit *his* body to its resting place; in firm and abiding faith that *he* doth now live in the life that is hereafter, and praying that thy love and peace may abide with *him*, this day and for evermore.

Unto Almighty God we commend the soul of our *brother* departed, and we commit *his* body to the elements; in sure and steadfast faith that, as *he* hath borne the image of the earthy, so also *he* doth now bear the image of the heavenly.

Unto Almighty God we commend the soul of our *brother* departed, and we commit *his* body to the deep; in sure and certain hope of the Resurrection unto eternal life, through our Lord Jesus Christ; at whose coming in glorious majesty to judge the world, the sea shall give up her dead; and the corruptible bodies of those who sleep in him shall be changed, and made like unto his glorious body; according to the mighty working whereby he is able to subdue all things unto himself.

Unto Almighty God, whose way is in the sea and paths in the great waters, we commend the soul of our *brother* departed, and we commit *his* body to the deep; in sure and certain faith that *he* doth now live in the life that is hereafter.

Into thy hands, O Lord, we commend the soul of thy departed servant, as unto a faithful Creator and most loving Redeemer; beseeching thee of thy great mercy to fulfill in *him* the purpose of thy love, and to bring us all to the joy of thy heavenly kingdom; through the merits of thy Son, our Savior Jesus Christ. *Amen.*

Believing that our *brother* is at rest in Christ, and rejoicing in the communion of saints, we commit *his* ashes to the ground (*or* their resting place *or* the waters), in sure and certain hope of the resurrection to eternal life, in the Presence of the Father, and of the Son, and of the Holy Spirit.

O Almighty and eternal God, in whose holy keeping are the souls of those who love thee: We again commit to the ground (*or* its resting place) the body of our *brother* departed; and we commend *his* soul to thy merciful care, praying that thou wilt grant unto *him* thy love and thy peace, now and for evermore.

O Almighty God, in whose eternal keeping are the souls of those who love thee: We commit these ashes of our *brother* departed to their resting place; in sure and certain faith that *he* doth now live in the life that is hereafter; and praying that *he* may grow in thy love and service, now and for evermore.

Benedictions

Unto God's gracious mercy and protection we commit
you. The LORD bless you and keep you. The LORD make
his face to shine upon you, and be gracious unto you.
The LORD lift up his countenance upon you, and give you
peace, both now and evermore. *Amen.*

And now may the blessing of the Lord rest and remain
upon all his people, in every land, of every tongue. The
Lord meet in mercy all that seek him. The Lord comfort all
that suffer and mourn. The Lord hasten his kindom,
and give you and all his people peace for evermore. *Amen.*

Go forth into the world in peace; be of good courage;
fight the good fight of faith; that ye may finish your course
with joy. And the blessing of God Almighty, the Father,
the Son, and the Holy Ghost, be upon you, and remain
with you for ever. *Amen.*

Now unto him who is able to keep you from falling, and
to present you faultless before the Presence of his glory,
with exceeding joy, to the only wise God, our Savior,
be glory and majesty, dominion and power, both now and
for evermore. *Amen.*

May the Father of all mercies, and God of all comfort,
support you in all your tribulations, that ye may be able
to strengthen those who are in any trouble, by the grace
wherewith ye yourselves are comforted of God. *Amen.*

May God the almighty direct your days in his peace, and grant you the gifts of his blessing; may he deliver you in all your troubles, and establish your minds in the tranquillity of his peace; and may he so guide you through things temporal, that ye finally lose not the things eternal, both now and for evermore. *Amen.*

May God bless you with a loving sense of his near Presence; guide, protect, and comfort you; that ye may know what it is to walk close with him all your life long, both here and hereafter. *Amen.*

Let us go forth in peace, with the comfort and consolation of Christ.
People Thanks be to God.

Special Burial Office for One for Whom the Prayer Book Office Is Not Appropriate

The Minister shall begin the Service by saying one or more of the Sentences following.

Enter not into judgment with thy servant, O Lord; for in thy sight shall no man living be justified.

To the Lord our God belong mercies and forgivenesses, though we have rebelled against him; neither have we obeyed the voice of the LORD our God, to walk in his laws which he set before us.

Let the wicked forsake his way, and the unrighteous man his thoughts: and let him return unto the LORD, and he will have mercy upon him; and to our God, for he will abundantly pardon.

O remember not the sins and offenses of my youth; but according to thy mercy think thou upon me, O LORD, for thy goodness.

God is our refuge and strength, a very present help in trouble.

Then shall be said one or more of the following Selections, taken from the Psalms.

Psalm 6 *Domine, ne in furore*

O LORD, rebuke me not in thine indignation, *
neither chasten me in thy displeasure.

Have mercy upon me, O LORD, for I am weak; *
LORD, heal me, for my bones are vexed.

My soul also is sore troubled: *
but, LORD, how long wilt thou punish me?

Turn thee, O LORD, and deliver my soul; *
O save me, for thy mercy's sake.

For in death no man remembereth thee; *
and who will give thee thanks in the pit?

I am weary of my groaning; *
every night wash I my bed,
and water my couch with my tears.

My beauty is gone for very trouble, *
and worn away because of all mine enemies.

Away from me, all ye that work iniquity; *
for the LORD hath heard the voice of my weeping.

The LORD hath heard my petition; *
the LORD will receive my prayer.

All mine enemies shall be confounded, and sore vexed; *
they shall be turned back, and put to shame suddenly.

Psalm 51 *Miserere mei, Deus*

Have mercy upon me, O God, after thy great goodness; *
according to the multitude of thy mercies do away
mine offenses.

Wash me throughly from my wickedness, *
  and cleanse me from my sin.

For I acknowledge my faults, *
  and my sin is ever before me.

Against thee only have I sinned, *
  and done this evil in thy sight:

That thou mightest be justified in thy saying, *
  and clear when thou shalt judge.

Behold, I was shapen in wickedness, *
  and in sin hath my mother conceived me.

But lo, thou requirest truth in the inward parts, *
  and shalt make me to understand wisdom secretly.

Thou shalt purge me with hyssop, and I shall be clean; *
  thou shalt wash me, and I shall be whiter than snow.

Thou shalt make me hear of joy and gladness, *
  that the bones which thou hast broken may rejoice.

Turn thy face from my sins, *
  and put out all my misdeeds.

Make me a clean heart, O God, *
  and renew a right spirit within me.

Cast me not away from thy presence, *
  and take not thy holy Spirit from me.

O give me the comfort of thy help again, *
  and stablish me with thy free Spirit.

Then shall I teach thy ways unto the wicked, *
  and sinners shall be converted unto thee.

Deliver me from blood-guiltiness, O God, *
    thou that art the God of my health;
    and my tongue shall sing of thy righteousness.

Thou shalt open my lips, O Lord, *
    and my mouth shall show thy praise.

For thou desirest no sacrifice, else would I give it thee; *
    but thou delightest not in burnt-offerings.

The sacrifice of God is a troubled spirit: *
    a broken and contrite heart, O God, shalt thou not despis

Psalm 103   *Benedic, anima mea*

The LORD is full of compassion and mercy, *
    long-suffering, and of great goodness.

He will not alway be chiding; *
    neither keepeth he his anger for ever.

He hath not dealt with us after our sins; *
    nor rewarded us according to our wickednesses.

For look how high the heaven is in comparison of the earth
    so great is his mercy also toward them that fear him.

Look how wide also the east is from the west; *
    so far hath he set our sins from us.

Yea, like as a father pitieth his own children; *
    even so is the LORD merciful unto them that fear him.

For he knoweth whereof we are made; *
    he remembereth that we are but dust.

The days of man are but as grass; *
    for he flourisheth as a flower of the field.

For as soon as the wind goeth over it, it is gone; *
  and the place thereof shall know it no more.

But the merciful goodness of the LORD endureth for ever
                  and ever upon them that fear him; *
  and his righteousness upon children's children;

Even upon such as keep his covenant, *
  and think upon his commandments to do them.

The LORD hath prepared his seat in heaven, *
  and his kingdom ruleth over all.

Psalm 130 *De profundis*

Out of the deep have I called unto thee, O LORD;
Lord, hear my voice. *
  O let thine ears consider well the voice of my complaint.

If thou, LORD, wilt be extreme to mark what is done amiss, *
  O Lord, who may abide it?

For there is mercy with thee; *
  therefore shalt thou be feared.

I look for the LORD; my soul doth wait for him; *
  in his word is my trust.

My soul fleeth unto the Lord
before the morning watch; *
  I say, before the morning watch.

O Israel, trust in the LORD, *
  for with the LORD there is mercy;

And with him is plenteous redemption, *
  and he shall redeem Israel from all his sins.

Psalm 143 *Domine, exaudi*

Hear my prayer, O LORD,
and consider my desire; *
   hearken unto me for thy truth and righteousness' sake.

And enter not into judgment with thy servant; *
   for in thy sight shall no man living be justified.

For the enemy hath persecuted my soul;
he hath smitten my life down to the ground; *
   he hath laid me in the darkness, as the men that have
           been long dead.

Therefore is my spirit vexed within me, *
   and my heart within me is desolate.

Yet do I remember the time past;
I muse upon all thy works; *
   yea, I exercise myself in the works of thy hands.

I stretch forth my hands unto thee; *
   my soul gaspeth unto thee as a thirsty land.

Hear me, O LORD, and that soon; for my spirit waxeth faint;
   hide not thy face from me,
   lest I be like unto them that go down into the pit.

O let me hear thy loving-kindness betimes in the morning;
for in thee is my trust; *
   show thou me the way that I should walk in;
   for I lift up my soul unto thee.

Deliver me, O LORD, from mine enemies; *
   for I flee unto thee to hide me.

Teach me to do the thing that pleaseth thee; for thou art my God;
   let thy loving Spirit lead me forth into the land
         of righteousness.

Quicken me, O LORD, for thy Name's sake; *
   and for thy righteousness' sake bring my soul out of trouble.

Then shall follow the Lesson.

Ecclesiastes 12:1-7, 13, 14

Remember now thy Creator in the days of thy youth, while
the evil days come not, nor the years draw nigh, when thou
shalt say, I have no pleasure in them; while the sun, or
the light, or the moon, or the stars, be not darkened, nor
the clouds return after the rain: in the day when the
keepers of the house shall tremble, and the strong men
shall bow themselves, and the grinders cease because
they are few, and those that look out of the windows be
darkened, and the doors shall be shut in the streets,
when the sound of the grinding is low, and he shall rise up
at the voice of the bird, and all the daughters of music
shall be brought low; also when they shall be afraid of that
which is high, and fears shall be in the way, and the
almond tree shall flourish, and the grasshopper shall be a
burden, and desire shall fail: because man goeth to his
long home, and the mourners go about the streets: or
ever the silver cord be loosed, or the golden bowl be broken,
or the pitcher be broken at the fountain, or the wheel
broken at the cistern. Then shall the dust return to the earth
as it was: and the spirit shall return unto God who gave
it. Let us hear the conclusion of the whole matter: Fear
God, and keep his commandments: for this is the whole
duty of man. For God shall bring every work into judgment,
with every secret thing, whether it be good, or whether
it be evil.

Then shall the Minister say such of the following, or other Prayers, as he may think fitting.

Let us pray.

Lord, have mercy upon us.
Christ, have mercy upon us.
Lord, have mercy upon us.

Our Father, who art in heaven, Hallowed be thy Name, Thy kingdom come, Thy will be done, On earth as it is in heaven. Give us this day our daily bread. And forgive us our trespasses, As we forgive those who trespass against us. And lead us not into temptation, But deliver us from evil. Amen.

Grant, we beseech thee, merciful Lord, to thy sinful creature a contrite and penitent heart; that he may be cleansed from all *his* sins, and, having obtained thy pardon and peace, may serve thee with a quiet mind in thy heavenly kingdom; through our Savior Jesus Christ. *Amen.*

O merciful Father, grant, we humbly beseech thee, unto the soul of this thy servant true repentance for all *his* sins; that *he* may obtain thy promised pardon and forgiveness, and grow in the knowledge and love of thee in the world that is hereafter, until *he* attain at last unto the stature of thy Son, Jesus Christ our Lord. *Amen.*

O heavenly Father, who dost send thy Holy Spirit to comfort the sorrowful, to strengthen the weak, and to guide those in perplexity: We beseech thee to look upon these thy servants in their sorrow, and to send to them the Holy Ghost the Comforter. Remember them, O Lord, in mercy, and console them by the manifestation of thy Presence;

endue their souls with patience under their affliction; comfort them with a sense of thy gracious goodness; lift up thy countenance upon them, and give them peace; through Jesus Christ our Lord. *Amen.*

Almighty God, who in the time of shadow and darkness canst be the only true and lasting light: Look upon thy sad children with thy constant mercy, and support them with thy loving strength; that they, casting all their care on thee, may have thy peace and consolation; through Jesus Christ our Lord. *Amen.*

Almighty God, who art ever ready to forgive, and to whom no prayer is made without hope of mercy: Speak to us thy word of consolation, as we draw near to thee under the shadow of this great affliction. Deepen within our hearts the assurance of thine unfailing compassion; deliver us from all bitterness, despair, and doubt of thy love; and grant us to know thy peace which passeth all understanding; through Jesus Christ our Lord. *Amen.*

Father of mercies and God of all comfort, who madest nothing in vain, and lovest all that thou hast made: Look in tender pity upon thy bereaved servants, that they may be enabled to find in thee their refuge and strength, and may be delivered out of their distress; through Jesus Christ our Lord. *Amen.*

O God, our only help in time of need: Watch with these thy people in their time of trouble, strengthen and quiet them with thy mercy; receive thy servant in *his* sudden death, and take *him* into thy holy keeping; through Jesus Christ our Lord. *Amen.*

O God, who knowest all our lights and all our shadows:
Look with compassion on this thy child who hath taken
his life with *his* own hand, and grant *him* true repentance
of *his* wilful deed, that thou mayest receive *him* as thine
own child. And, we pray thee, deal graciously with those
who love *him*, and grant that in all their troubles they
may know thy healing and redeeming love, made known
to us in Christ Jesus our Lord. *Amen.*

Almighty God, give us grace that we may cast away the
works of darkness, and put upon us the armor of light,
now in the time of this mortal life, in which thy Son
Jesus Christ came to visit us in great humility; that in the
last day, when he shall come again in his glorious majesty
to judge both the quick and the dead, we may rise to
the life immortal, through him who liveth and reigneth
with thee and the Holy Ghost, now and ever. *Amen.*

O Lord, we beseech thee, absolve thy people from their
offenses; that through thy bountiful goodness we may
all be delivered from the bands of those sins, which by our
frailty we have committed. Grant this, O heavenly Father,
for the sake of Jesus Christ, our blessed Lord and Savior.
Amen.

Almighty God, who showest to them that are in error the
light of thy truth, to the intent that they may return into
the way of righteousness: Grant unto all those who are
admitted into the fellowship of Christ's Religion, that
they may avoid those things that are contrary to their
profession, and follow all such things as are agreeable to
the same; through our Lord Jesus Christ. *Amen.*

Almighty and everlasting God, who art always more ready to hear than we to pray, and art wont to give more than either we desire or deserve: Pour down upon us the abundance of thy mercy; forgiving us those things whereof our conscience is afraid, and giving us those good things which we are not worthy to ask, but through the merits and mediation of Jesus Christ, thy Son, our Lord. *Amen.*

Almighty God, the fountain of all wisdom, who knowest our necessities before we ask, and our ignorance in asking: We beseech thee to have compassion upon our infirmities; and those things which for our unworthiness we dare not, and for our blindness we cannot ask, vouchsafe to give us, for the worthiness of thy Son Jesus Christ our Lord. *Amen.*

The grace of our Lord Jesus Christ, and the love of God, and the fellowship of the Holy Ghost, be with us all evermore. *Amen.*

When they come to the Grave, while the Body is made ready to be laid into the earth, shall be said,

Man, that is born of a woman, hath but a short time to live, and is full of misery. He cometh up, and is cut down, like a flower; he fleeth as it were a shadow, and never continueth in one stay.

In the midst of life we are in death; of whom may we seek for succor, but of thee, O Lord, who for our sins art justly displeased?

Yet, O Lord God most holy, O Lord most mighty, O holy and most merciful Savior, deliver us not into the bitter pains of eternal death.

Thou knowest, Lord, the secrets of our hearts; shut not thy merciful ears to our prayer; but spare us, Lord most holy, O God most mighty, O holy and merciful Savior, thou most worthy Judge eternal, suffer us not, at our last hour, for any pains of death, to fall from thee.

Then, while the earth shall be cast upon the Body by some standing by, the Minister shall say

Unto the mercies of God Almighty we commend the soul of our *brother* departed, and we commit *his* body to the ground; earth to earth, ashes to ashes, dust to dust; praying that, as *he* hath borne the image of the earthy, so also *he* may be found worthy to bear the image of the heavenly.

or this

Eternal God, with whom there is mercy and plenteous redemption: We commend to thy love and keeping the soul of this our *brother*, and we commit *his* body to the ground, earth to earth, ashes to ashes, dust to dust. And we pray that by the most precious death and passion of thy dear Son, and sharing in the riches of his grace, both this our *brother* and we may at the last be found acceptable in thy sight; through Jesus Christ our only Savior and Advocate. *Amen.*

Or else, where the Body is to be cremated, the Minister shall say

Unto the mercies of God Almighty we commend the soul of our *brother* departed, and we commit *his* body to the elements; praying that, as *he* hath borne the image of the earthy, so also *he* may be found worthy to bear the image of the heavenly.

Then shall be said

Thou, O Lord God, art full of compassion and mercy, long-suffering, plenteous in goodness and truth. O turn thee then unto us, and have mercy upon us; give thy strength unto thy servant, and help the *son* of thine handmaid.

Then the Minister shall say one or more of the following Prayers, at his discretion.

Let us pray.

O Lord, in thine infinite mercy, do thou so cleanse and purify the soul of this thy servant, that *he*, turning unto thee and being pardoned from *his* sins, may go from strength to strength, and serve thee faithfully in thy heavenly kingdom; through Jesus Christ our Lord. *Amen.*

Almighty God, Creator of all mankind, have mercy on all those who in their darkness have thrown away their mortal lives. Grant them penitence, light, and salvation, that they may find new life in thy love, and glorify thy holy Name; through Jesus Christ our Lord. *Amen.*

Our heavenly Father, we pray thee to be with these thy servants in their sorrow; and so turn their hearts unto thee, that, abiding in thy Presence, they may be comforted by thy consoling love; through Jesus Christ our Lord. *Amen.*

O Lord Jesus Christ, who didst weep at the grave of Lazarus thy friend: Have compassion upon thy servants who mourn this untimely death; and hasten the time when sin and sorrow shall be no more, and all shall rejoice in thee, the Resurrection and the Life; who with the Father and the Holy Spirit livest and reignest one God, world without end. *Amen.*

We humbly beseech thee, O Father, mercifully to look upon our infirmities; and, for the glory of thy Name, turn from us all those evils that we most justly have deserved; and grant, that in all our troubles we may put our whole trust and confidence in thy mercy, and evermore serve thee in holiness and pureness of living, to thy honor and glory; through our only Mediator and Advocate, Jesus Christ our Lord. *Amen.*

May grace, mercy, and peace from God Almighty, the Father, the Son, and the Holy Ghost, be with you and abide with you, now and for evermore. *Amen.*

Burial of One Who Does Not Profess the Christian Faith

This anthem; and any of the following Psalms, Lessons, Prayers; and the form of Committal given below may be used with the Order for Burial on page 88.

Opening Anthem

The steadfast love of the Lord never ceases,
his mercies never come to an end;
they are new every morning;
great is his faithfulness.
The Lord will not cast off for ever.
Though he cause grief, he will have compassion
according to the abundance of his steadfast love;
The Lord does not willingly afflict or grieve his children.

Lessons and Psalms

Ecclesiastes 3:1-11

For everything its season, and for every activity under heaven its time: a time to be born and a time to die; a time to plant and a time to uproot; a time to kill and a time to heal; a time to pull down and a time to build up; a time to weep and a time to laugh; a time for mourning and

a time for dancing; a time to scatter stones and a time to
gather them; a time to embrace and a time to refrain
from embracing; a time to seek and a time to lose; a time
to keep and a time to throw away; a time to tear and
a time to mend; a time for silence and a time for speech; a
time to love and a time to hate; a time for war and a
time for peace. What profit does one who works get from
all his labour? I have seen the business that God has given
men to keep them busy. He has made everything to suit
its time; moreover he has given men a sense of time past
and future, but no comprehension of God's work from
beginning to end.

Ecclesiastes 12:1-7

Remember your Creator in the days of your youth, before
the time of trouble comes and the years draw near when
you will say, 'I see no purpose in them.' Remember him
before the sun and the light of day give place to darkness,
before the moon and the stars grow dim, and the clouds
return with the rain—when the guardians of the house
tremble, and the strong men stoop, when the women grinding
the meal cease work because they are few, and those
who look through the windows look no longer, when the
street-doors are shut, when the noise of the mill is low,
when the chirping of the sparrow grows faint and the
song-birds fall silent; when men are afraid of a steep place
and the street is full of terrors, when the blossom whitens
on the almond-tree and the locust's paunch is swollen
and caper-buds have no more zest. For man goes to his
everlasting home, and the mourners go about the streets.
Remember him before the silver cord is snapped and
the golden bowl is broken, before the pitcher is shattered
at the spring and the wheel broken at the well, before
the dust returns to the earth as it began and the spirit returns
to God who gave it.

Psalm 23   *(King James Version)*

The LORD is my shepherd; *
   I shall not want.

He maketh me to lie down in green pastures; *
   he leadeth me beside the still waters.

He restoreth my soul; *
   he leadeth me in the paths of righteousness for his
          Name's sake.

Yea, though I walk through the valley of the shadow of death,
I will fear no evil; *
   for thou art with me;
   thy rod and thy staff, they comfort me.

Thou preparest a table before me in the presence of
          mine enemies; *
   thou anointest my head with oil;
   my cup runneth over.

Surely goodness and mercy shall follow me all the days
          of my life, *
   and I will dwell in the house of the LORD for ever.

Psalm 90   *Domine, refugium*

Lord, you have been our refuge *
   from one generation to another.

Before the mountains were brought forth,
or the land and the earth were born, *
   from age to age you are God.

You turn us back to the dust and say, *
   "Go back, O child of earth."

For a thousand years in your sight are like yesterday
          when it is past *
  and like a watch in the night.

You sweep us away like a dream; *
  we fade away suddenly like the grass.

In the morning it is green and flourishes; *
  in the evening it is dried up and withered.

For we consume away in your displeasure; *
  we are afraid because of your wrathful indignation.

Our iniquities you have set before you, *
  and our secret sins in the light of your countenance.

When you are angry, all our days are gone; *
  we bring our years to an end like a sigh.

The span of our life is seventy years,
perhaps in strength even eighty; *
  yet the sum of them is but labor and sorrow,
  for they pass away quickly and we are gone.

Who regards the power of your wrath? *
  who rightly fears your indignation?

So teach us to number our days *
  that we may apply our hearts to wisdom.

Psalm 121   *Levavi oculos*

I lift up my eyes to the hills; *
  from where is my help to come?

My help comes from the LORD, *
  the maker of heaven and earth.

He will not let your foot be moved *
  and he who watches over you will not fall asleep.

190   Burial of a Non-Christian

Behold, he who keeps watch over Israel *
  shall neither slumber nor sleep;

The LORD himself watches over you; *
  the LORD is your shade at your right hand,

So that the sun shall not strike you by day, *
  nor the moon by night.

The LORD shall preserve you from all evil; *
  it is he who shall keep you safe.

The LORD shall watch over your going out and
                    your coming in, *
  from this time forth for evermore.

Psalm 130 *De profundis*

Out of the depths have I called to you, O LORD;
Lord, hear my voice; *
  let your ears consider well the voice of my supplication.

If you, LORD, were to note what is done amiss, *
  O Lord, who could stand?

For there is forgiveness with you; *
  therefore you shall be feared.

I wait for the LORD; my soul waits for him; *
  in his word is my hope.

My soul waits for the Lord,
more than watchmen for the morning, *
  more than watchmen for the morning.

O Israel, wait for the LORD, *
  for with the LORD there is mercy;

With him there is plenteous redemption, *
  and he shall redeem Israel from all their sins.

Romans 8:35-39

What can separate us from the love of Christ? Can affliction
or hardship? Can persecution, hunger, nakedness, peril,
or the sword? 'We are being done to death for thy sake all
day long,' as Scripture says; 'we have been treated like sheep
for slaughter'—and yet, in spite of all, overwhelming
victory is ours through him who loved us. For I am convinced
that there is nothing in death or life, in the realm of spirits
or superhuman powers, in the world as it is or the world
as it shall be, in the forces of the universe, in heights
or depths—nothing in all creation that can separate us from
the love of God in Christ Jesus our Lord.

John 10:11-16

'I am the good shepherd; the good shepherd lays down his
life for the sheep. The hireling, when he sees the wolf
coming, abandons the sheep and runs away, because he is
no shepherd and the sheep are not his. Then the wolf
harries the flock and scatters the sheep. The man runs away
because he is a hireling and cares nothing for the sheep.
I am the good shepherd; I know my own sheep and my
sheep know me—as the Father knows me and I know the
Father—and I lay down my life for the sheep. But there
are other sheep of mine, not belonging to this fold, whom
I must bring in; and they too will listen to my voice.
There will then be one flock, one shepherd.'

Prayers

For the Deceased

Almighty God, we entrust all who are dear to us to your
never-failing care and love, for this life and the life to
come, knowing that you are doing for them better things

than we can desire or pray for; through Jesus Christ our Lord. *Amen.*

Into your hands, O God, we commend our *brother, N.,* as into the hands of a faithful Creator and most loving Savior. In your infinite goodness, wisdom, and power, work in *him* the merciful purpose of your perfect will; through Jesus Christ our Lord. *Amen.*

For those who mourn

O God of grace and glory, we remember before you this day our brother (sister), *N.* We thank you for giving *him* to us, *his* family and friends, to know and to love as a companion on our earthly pilgrimage. In your boundless compassion, console us who mourn. Give us quiet confidence that we may continue our course in faith; through Jesus Christ our Lord. *Amen.*

O merciful Father, you have taught us in your holy Word that you do not willingly afflict or grieve your children: Look with pity upon the sorrows of your servants for whom our prayers are offered. Remember them, O Lord, in mercy, nourish their souls with patience, comfort them with a sense of your goodness, lift up your countenance upon them, and give them peace; through Jesus Christ our Lord. *Amen.*

Almighty God, Father of mercies and giver of comfort: Deal graciously, we pray, with all who mourn; that, casting all their care on you, they may know the consolation of your love; through Jesus Christ our Lord. *Amen.*

Most merciful God, whose wisdom is beyond our understanding, deal graciously with *NN.* in *their* grief. Surround *them* with your love, that *they* may not be overwhelmed by *their* loss, but have confidence in your goodness, and strength to meet the days to come; through Jesus Christ our Lord. *Amen.*

For the Christian community

Most loving Father, whose will it is for us to give thanks for all things, to fear nothing but the loss of you, and to cast all our care on you who care for us: Preserve us from faithless fears and worldly anxieties, that no clouds of this mortal life may hide from us the light of that love which is immortal, and which you have manifested to us in your Son Jesus Christ our Lord. *Amen.*

Almighty God, give us grace to cast away the works of darkness, and put on the armor of light, now in the time of this mortal life in which your Son Jesus Christ came to visit us in great humility; that in the last day, when he shall come again in his glorious majesty to judge both the living and the dead, we may rise to the life immortal; through him who lives and reigns for ever and ever. *Amen.*

The Committal

Holy God, Holy and Mighty, Holy Immortal One, have mercy upon us.

You only are immortal, the creator and maker of mankind; and we are mortal, formed of the earth, and to earth shall we return. For so did you ordain when you created me, saying, "You are dust, and to dust you shall return." All of us go down to the dust; yet even at the grave we make our song: Alleluia, alleluia, alleluia.

Holy God, Holy and Mighty, Holy Immortal One, have mercy upon us.

Ministration at the Time of Death

When a person is near death, the Minister of the Congregation should be notified, in order that the ministrations of the Church may be provided.

A Prayer for a Person near Death

Almighty God, look on this your servant, lying in great weakness, and comfort *him* with the promise of life everlasting, given in the resurrection of your Son Jesus Christ our Lord. *Amen.*

Litany at the Time of Death

When possible, it is desirable that members of the family and friends come together to join in the Litany.

God the Father,
Have mercy on your servant.

God the Son,
Have mercy on your servant.

God the Holy Spirit,
Have mercy on your servant.

Holy Trinity, one God,
Have mercy on your servant.

From all evil, from all sin, from all tribulation,
Good Lord, deliver him.

By your holy Incarnation, by your Cross and Passion, by
your precious Death and Burial,
Good Lord, deliver him.

By your glorious Resurrection and Ascension, and by the
Coming of the Holy Spirit,
Good Lord, deliver him.

We sinners beseech you to hear us, Lord Christ: That it may
please you to deliver the soul of your servant from the power
of evil, and from eternal death,
We beseech you to hear us, good Lord.

That it may please you mercifully to pardon all *his* sins,
We beseech you to hear us, good Lord.

That it may please you to grant *him* a place of refreshment
and everlasting blessedness,
We beseech you to hear us, good Lord.

That it may please you to give *him* joy and gladness in your
kingdom, with your saints in light,
We beseech you to hear us, good Lord.

Jesus, Lamb of God:
Have mercy on him.

Jesus, bearer of our sins:
Have mercy on him.

Jesus, redeemer of the world:
Give him *your peace.*

Lord, have mercy.
Christ, have mercy.
Lord, have mercy.

Officiant and People

Our Father, who art in heaven,	Our Father in heaven,
hallowed be thy Name,	hallowed be your Name,
thy kingdom come,	your kingdom come,
thy will be done,	your will be done,
on earth as it is in heaven.	on earth as in heaven.
Give us this day our daily bread.	Give us today our daily bread.
And forgive us our trespasses,	Forgive us our sins
as we forgive those	as we forgive those
who trespass against us.	who sin against us.
And lead us not into temptation,	Save us from the time of trial,
but deliver us from evil.	and deliver us from evil.

The Officiant says this Collect

Let us pray.

Deliver your servant, *N.*, O Sovereign Lord Christ, from all evil, and set *him* free from every bond; that *he* may rest with all your saints in the eternal habitations; where with the Father and the Holy Spirit you live and reign, one God, for ever and ever. *Amen.*

A Commendation at the Time of Death

Depart, O Christian soul, out of this world;
In the Name of God the Father Almighty who created you;
In the Name of Jesus Christ who redeemed you;
In the Name of the Holy Spirit who sanctifies you.
May your rest be this day in peace,
and your dwelling place in the Paradise of God.

A Commendatory Prayer

Into your hands, O merciful Savior, we commend your
servant N. Acknowledge, we humbly beseech you, a
sheep of your own fold, a lamb of your own flock, a sinner
of your own redeeming. Receive *him* into the arms of
your mercy, into the blessed rest of everlasting peace, and
into the glorious company of the saints in light. *Amen.*

May *his* soul and the souls of all the departed, through the
mercy of God, rest in peace. *Amen.*

Prayers for a Vigil

*It is appropriate that the family and friends come together for prayers
prior to the funeral. Suitable Psalms, Lessons, and Collects (such
as those in the Burial service) may be used. The Litany at the Time of
Death may be said, or the following*

Dear Friends: It was our Lord Jesus himself who said,
"Come to me, all you who labor and are burdened, and I
will give you rest." Let us pray, then, for our brother
(sister), N., that *he* may rest from *his* labors, and enter
into the light of God's eternal sabbath rest.

Receive, O Lord, your servant, for *he* returns to you.
Into your hands, O Lord,
we commend our brother (sister) N.

Wash *him* in the holy font of everlasting life, and clothe
him in *his* heavenly wedding garment.
Into your hands, O Lord,
we commend our brother (sister) N.

May *he* hear your words of invitation, "Come, you
blessed of my Father."
Into your hands, O Lord,
we commend our brother (sister) N.

May *he* gaze upon you, Lord, face to face, and taste the blessedness of perfect rest.
Into your hands, O Lord,
we commend our brother (sister) N.

May angels surround *him,* and saints welcome *him* in peace.
Into your hands, O Lord,
we commend our brother (sister) N.

The Officiant concludes

Almighty God, our Father in heaven, before whom live all who die in the Lord: Receive our *brother N.* into the courts of your heavenly dwelling place. Let *his* heart and soul now ring out in joy to you, O Lord, the living God, and the God of those who live. This we ask through Christ our Lord. *Amen.*

Reception of the Body

The following form may be used at whatever time the body is brought to the church.

The Celebrant meets the body at the door of the church and says

With faith in Jesus Christ, we receive the body of our brother (sister) *N.* for burial. Let us pray with confidence to God, the Giver of life, that he will raise *him* to perfection in the company of the saints.

Silence may be kept; after which the Celebrant says

Deliver your servant, *N.,* O Sovereign Lord Christ, from all evil, and set *him* free from every bond; that *he* may rest with all your saints in the eternal habitations; where with the Father and the Holy Spirit you live and reign, one God, for ever and ever. *Amen.*

Let us also pray for all who mourn, that they may cast their care on God, and know the consolation of his love.

Silence may be kept; after which the Celebrant says

Almighty God, look with pity upon the sorrows of your servants for whom we pray. Remember them, Lord, in mercy; nourish them with patience; comfort them with a sense of your goodness; lift up your countenance upon them; and give them peace; through Jesus Christ our Lord. *Amen.*

If the Burial service is not to follow immediately, the body is then brought into the church, during which time a suitable psalm or anthem may be sung or said. Appropriate devotions, such as those appointed for the Vigil on page 198, may follow.

When the order for the Burial of the Dead follows immediately, the service continues on page 11 or 51.

A member of the congregation bearing the lighted Paschal Candle may lead the procession into the church.